D1609022

AMERICAN GRAPHIC QUILT DESIGNS

★★★ DOLORES A. HINSON ★★★

ARCO PUBLISHING, INC.
NEW YORK

*To my mother, Iris Codling, who was my earliest instructor
in appreciating the things around me that were made
by loving hands.*

NOTE TO THE READER

It is recommended that you test your patterns before cutting any cloth. Do this by tracing the pattern pieces in the exact arrangement in which they will be sewn onto a piece of paper the size of the finished block. Make sure that all the pattern pieces fit together properly: use a pencil and ruler to make any minor adjustments. If you alter any pattern pieces, retrace the entire block on another piece of paper to double-check the arrangement. After making any necessary adjustments, cut the final cardboard cutting patterns and begin tracing your patterns on cloth.

Published by Arco Publishing, Inc.
215 Park Avenue South, New York, N.Y. 10003

Copyright © 1983 by Dolores Hinson

Library of Congress Cataloging in Publication Data

Hinson, Dolores A.
  American graphic quilt designs.

  1. Quilting—United States—Patterns.   I. Title.
TT835.H46   746.9'7041   82-3901
ISBN 0-668-05262-7   AACR2

Printed in the United States of America

10 9 8 7 6 5 4 3 2 1

Contents

Acknowledgments

This book has been a joy to write, both in the original gathering of the material and in actually putting this material into a book. Each new-found quilt offered its own beauty and brought a new shade of meaning to the work. I have benefited from the help and interest of many people. At this time I wish to thank these people and acknowledge that without them, this book probably never would have been written:

Miss Bowman of the Textile Division and Mrs. Steel of the Index of American Design, National Gallery of Art, Washington, D.C.; Mr. Johnson, Curator of the DAR Museum, Washington, D.C.; Mr. Greene of the Shelburne Museum, Shelburne, Vermont; the Philadelphia Art Museum, Philadelphia, Pennsylvania; and the Art Museum of St. Louis, St. Louis, Missouri. I also wish to thank all of the people who brought me their quilts to study and the people who told me about quilts they had seen, which made gathering material for this book much easier.

Quilt friends who spent much time and effort on behalf of this book are Mrs. Cuesta Benberry of St. Louis, Missouri, and Mrs. Mary Schafer of Flushing, Michigan. My mother, Iris Codling, and our good friend, Charlotte Walker, helped me in checking for errors and did the preliminary editing.

Patterns and Directions

Five of the quilts in this book are accompanied by their patterns. These patterns are given in the traditional way, which means that the outlines of the finished pattern pieces are given without the seam allowances. In other words, these pieces are the finished size. Trace these patterns from the book page onto tissue paper.[1] Cut out the tissue pattern and traced this outline onto plastic, sandpaper, cardboard, or other heavy pattern material. Use these heavy patterns to trace the outlines onto the cloth chosen for the quilt with a lightly penciled line. For dark fabrics, use a white photography pencil, available at most stationery stores. When tracing patterns onto the cloth, leave one-half-inch spaces between the outlines. Cut the patterns apart by cutting down the center of the half-inch spaces, leaving one-fourth-inch seam allowances around each cloth motif. Seam allowances, whenever they are rounded or end in sharp angles, should be clipped closely, almost to the penciled lines.

Appliqué the motifs using a blind stitch, also called a hem stitch. The smaller the stitch used and the less the stitches show, the more your finished quilt will look like the antique models. Use any of the blocks given, in any order, or use the separate motifs given in the patterns to put together your own quilt patches.

You may copy any of the quilts exactly, but 19th-century needlewomen made their quilts to suit their feelings at the time. The old saying is that they "cut their patches to suit their cloth," meaning that they used whatever was available at the moment and trusted intuition to give them subjects for their blocks.

Color Chart for Author's Drawings

In my drawings, I have tried to make the colors of the quilts clearer by using different shadings for each color. Some colors are the same value of gray, so the shading in the cross-hatching is the same. For those shades you will have to check the text, which will give the colors used in each quilt (where I have been able to obtain that information). The closer the cross-hatching is, the darker the color represented.

[1] See the instructions on page ii

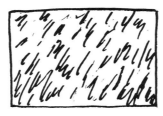

Very loose cross-hatching is orange, gold, or dark yellow

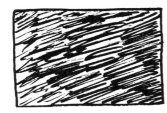

Loosely cross-hatched is pink or tan

Solid black is either red or black

Straight lines are always green

Closely cross-hatched is rose or brown

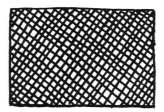

Cross-hatched both ways is always a shade of blue

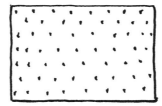

Dotted is always yellow

Squiggly lines are purple or a print too small and close together to be easily reproduced

1

Origins of the
American Graphic Quilt

About ten years ago, a quilt in Pennsylvania, which was very similar to the best quilts shown in this book, was sold at auction. The final bid of $38,000.00 was from the agent of a Texas man who wanted a beautiful quilt to set off a bed in his antique collection. Of course, a product of one of the minor crafts is seldom given such a vote of confidence. The quilt brought a huge price only because it was an authentic antique.

I am writing this book about the quilt as an art and craft form. As a group, the most beautiful quilts ever made are the ones I call American graphic quilts, for want of a better name. These quilts are outstanding in that no two blocks on any one quilt are ever just alike.

The first American graphic quilts were made either in Baltimore or by the surrounding society of the Chesapeake Bay and the allied river systems. From there, this style spread to the North, through Pennsylvania, New York, and Ohio, and on across the country wherever women had enough leisure time to do truly fine, imaginative needlework. Today, museums that have one or two examples of this fine work consider themselves very lucky. Women today have the leisure for fine needlework if they wish. Any artist or craftswoman should consider taking up the cloth arts.

When you look at the drawings of the quilts used in this book, you will notice that there are quilts which have been called Album, Friendship, Bride's, Presentation, Medley, and many other similar names. Unless the origin of a quilt has been handed down in the family along with the quilt, it is often hard to decide whether a quilt should be considered a Bride's quilt, a Friendship quilt, an Album quilt, or whether it falls under one of the different headings of these classes. The definitions for these headings, as far as I can work them out from the rules of folk art, are:

Album Quilts — This quilt was usually made from blocks, each designed and worked by a different person at home. The blocks were then brought to a quilting party where they were sewn together into a top, which was then quilted, also through joint effort. The blocks can be of many sizes and colors and some may not match very well. Under this general description, there are several subheadings:

1. Signature quilts, which have dates and the signature of the maker in each block.
2. Autograph quilts, which have the maker's name and perhaps a favorite motto on the blocks.
3. Bible quilts, which have the name of the maker and a favorite Bible verse or verse number on the blocks. There are other variations, such as poetry quilts and quilts made with favorite passages from classical literature.

Quilts made by churches and other groups to raise money are also considered Album quilts. These had sections marked out on each block and the sections were sold for a nominal fee; one dollar was a typical fee in the 1930s. The buyer wrote his name in his section and the person in charge of that block embroidered the name. Usually, more money was obtained by raffling off the finished quilt within the organization.

Bride's Quilts — This quilt was often made by an engaged woman to represent her very best work. Alternatively, a Bride's quilt was made by friends of the bride-to-be at an engagement party. Each block was signed by its maker. The second kind of Bride's quilt evolved a little later than the first. In either case, the quilt was to be used as a spread on the marriage bed. A Bride's quilt can sometimes be identified by blocks that have heart-shaped designs or elements, when the quilt is not otherwise labeled. Hearts were not usually used in other 19th-century quilts.

Friendship Quilts — This quilt was made at a party for one of the members of the group. Such quilts were signed by all of the members, and could be made for any occasion, including a wedding. Earlier Friendship quilts are usually more pleasing in design than later ones, because the quilters brought their cloth to the party and pieced the designs there, setting the finished blocks together and quilting them before the evening was over. Thus they were able to assemble designs for their blocks that made a harmonious quilt top. After the middle of the 19th century, the tendency was for each quilter to make a favorite pattern into a block at home. All the quilters then met at a party and set the blocks together, quilting the resulting top and presenting the finished quilt as before.

The modern Friendship quilt is made by asking several people to make a block of a certain size. This block may give the maker's name and the date or other information such as the maker's birthday, marriage anniversary, or address. Friendship quilts are most popular among groups of pen pals, who usually attempt a quilt with blocks from all fifty states or from many different countries. A party has no part in making this quilt, as the blocks are usually mailed to the owner, who then pieces the blocks into her own quilt.

Medley Quilts — These quilts are made up of the favorite quilt block patterns of the maker, and are made by one or at the most two people for themselves.

Picture Quilts — These are quilts whose block designs have become frankly pictorial. They are usually made by one individual. Sometimes blocks are combined to tell a simple story. In the 19th century, most of these quilts were religious or political in nature, and they were most popular in the latter half of the century. Today, they usually take the form of children's story quilts, although I have seen a pattern for a *Gone With the Wind* quilt.

Presentation Quilts — This kind of quilt was made

by a group, usually at a party, to be presented to a person who was being honored by the group. Presentation quilts were made for special occasions, such as a minister's retirement or departure from his congregation, a well-liked man's acceptance of promotion or political position, or a family's move from the area. President Zachary Taylor received a commemorative quilt from the "Ladies of Baltimore" when he attended a fair in that city in 1849. A few years later, the women of several rural churches gave their retiring minister a quilt, now famous, called "The Circuit Rider." This quilt is now in the collection of the Chicago Art Institute. The Captain Russell Quilt, discussed in Chapter 5, is also a Presentation quilt.

All of the quilts discussed above are one-of-a-kind quilts, with several differences from quilt to quilt even where the designs are very similar. I have tried to find the present location and owner of each quilt described in this book, but in some cases where the information was obtained from a 1930s magazine or newspaper article or from sketches in the Index of American Design, the quilts themselves cannot be found. Permission to use quilt drawings from the Index was obtained from the Index of American Design, National Gallery of Art, Washington, D.C.

All other credits are given in the captions for the drawings and photographs.

A General History of American Graphic Quilts

Sometime early in the 18th century, Southern ladies began to make a quilt called a Medallion quilt. It combined European quilts, the pieced scrap quilts of the North, and the elaborate appliqué quilts made for show by very wealthy ladies in the South. The Medallion quilt deserves to have its story told separately because of its many variations and long popularity in the Eastern states both before and just after the Revolutionary War. I will save these quilts for another book. The American graphic quilts evolved directly from these Medallion quilts, after dropping some of the European influence and taking more from the Northern block quilts. The block arrangement of the earliest American graphic quilts shows their Medallion origins very clearly (*See* Picture 5 in Chapter 2).

To understand the origins of the designs used in these quilts, a little knowledge of the history and theory of crafts is helpful. Because crafts and the hand arts have always been passed down by the apprentice method — from mother to daughter, father to son, master craftsman to young apprentice — there are neither hard-and-fast ways of doing handwork, nor patterns and designs that must be used, as there are in more systematic disciplines. If it looks right, do it that way. If the pattern is pleasing, use it. Thus, the patterns for hooked rugs are also found in crewelwork; crewelwork patterns are seen on hand-painted china, and china patterns are used in quilts. Who cares where the pattern came from or where it was used last? If you like it, use it.

In the 1830s, the first women's magazines were published in this country. Their contents ranged from literature and fashion to health articles to music for the parlor organ. Actually, they had the same kinds of articles as are found in these magazines today. From the start, simple embroidery patterns appeared in these magazines and the designs were often embellished and converted into larger patterns which could be used in rugs, quilts, and needlepoint.

Also at this time, many small books containing designs and patterns for needlework were published in this country and abroad. Another probable design source was woodcut fillers. These designs were cut in wood stamps and often depicted ships, horses, or baskets of fruit and flowers. These stamps were used to decorate and fill the blank spaces in the newspapers of that era. I have included one design from a ladies' magazine and one of the woodcut fillers from early in the 19th century (*See* Figures 1 and 2). This woodcut shows an appliqué motif typical of American graphic quilts, especially the Baltimore style patterns: fruit divided into equal halves with a light and a dark side. Oval leaves and leaves divided in half with two shades of green are also shown.

The people and things the quilters lived with provided a third inspiration for original quilt patterns. In Chapter 9, I have enlarged a block showing a man being thrown from a horse (*See* Picture 63). This incident must be one that really took place. There is a teasing quality in the caricature of the man's face that tells me that the quilter was having a good laugh at someone's expense. In the book *Wide Meadows* by Jean Bell Mosely, part of one section tells about quilts that were inspired entirely by incidents that happened around the farm home of the quilter. The chapter is called "A Gift for Molly," and here is the passage:[1]

Over grandmother's "Passage of Time Quilts" Molly went into ecstasies. These quilts were Grandma's way of keeping a history of the family and friends. There were 24 blocks to a quilt, each one depicting in appliqué and embroidery the most interesting events that happened in our lives as time went by. She drafted her own designs for she was good at drawing, and sometimes the completed block would be intricate beyond all reason and as complicated as a mosaic tile. Take the time the bull butted Grandpa into the river and jumped in after him. There were three scenes in this one block — Grandpa standing on the riverbank fishing; Grandpa halfway across the river, the bull in hot pursuit; and Grandpa climbing a tree on the other side, water dripping from his clothing in the form of blue French knots and with a satin stitch blue jay perched in the tree watching.

Sometimes we chided Grandma about her drawings. The barn didn't sway in the middle the way ours really did and in the block where she had me in the swing, the tree was generously foliaged and well-proportioned instead of a spindly old walnut.

"Well, I draw them like they look to me," Grandma would say, and that seemed reason enough.

Regional styles in quilting are also significant in the study of these quilts. A regional style grew and developed from the life style of people living in that region and whether or not quilts were needed for warmth. To a lesser degree, the affluence of the maker's family and her training or lack of it modified her use of the regional styles.

The plainest and most utilitarian quilts were made in New England, where, with the great practical need for quilts, there was no time for elaboration. Almost all New England quilts and patterns were pieced.

The New York-New Jersey style (hereafter called the NY-NJ style) is another regional style. The very popular mid-19th-century fad of green and red on white quilts originated in the NY-NJ area, and then spread to the rest of the country. There were both pieced and appliquéd quilts in this area, reflecting

[1]Jean Bell Mosely, *Wide Meadows* (Caldwell, Idaho: Caxton Printers, 1960).

Figure 1 Floral appliqué design given in *Godey's Ladies Magazine.*

Figure 2 Basket of fruit taken from a printer's woodcut filler.

4

the influence of both the New England quilters and those farther south. The patterns are quite regular and balanced even in the appliquéd designs. An example of this style is shown in Picture 1.

A third regional style is that of Tidewater, Maryland. The style spread to bordering states accessible by water. This style will be discussed fully in the chapters which follow under the heading of

Picture 1 NY-NJ style quilt, mostly red and green cloth appliquéd on white. This quilt shows the same influence as do the Baltimore-style quilts, though changed by regional quilting traditions. Courtesy Shelburne Museum, Shelburne, Vermont.

the Baltimore-style quilt. An early Baltimore-style quilt is shown in Picture 2.

A fourth style is that of the Deep South. In these warmer areas, quilts were not needed in any quantity and much attention could be lavished on elaborating the designs. These quilts are almost always appliquéd.

The regional styles of Maryland and the Deep South, however, are not exclusive in these regions. The quilts made in the inland and mountain areas of these regions seem to reflect economic and social ties with the states farther north, rather than with the seacoast areas of their own parts of the country. Thus, the inland Maryland and Appalachian Mountain quilts are more often pieced work than appliqué and the patterns have much in common with the NY-NJ style quilts. In the more remote and poorer sections of the southern mountains, the quilts resemble New England quilts in their plain patterns, differing from the northern quilts only in the use of more and brighter colors.

Another important influence on the American graphic quilt designs was the patterns used in some of the larger and brighter chintz fabrics of the late 18th and early 19th centuries. The quilt shown in Picture 3 is one of the most beautiful of the quilts made from cutout chintz cloth designs that I have found. The printed designs are cut from the cloth and appliquéd to a background square. Since chintz cloth was printed in an overall design, fine discrimination was needed to cut out a part of the pattern from a section of the cloth and use it to make a pretty quilt square. Strips of striped chintz have been cut out and used for the lattice strips and wide borders of this quilt. Many of the block designs in American graphic quilts show that they were originally inspired by chintz cloth patterns. Designs from the painted cotton cloths brought from India, called Palampore, were also adapted, although these cloths are much more famous for having inspired the Jacobean crewel embroidery of the 17th and 18th centuries.

I think that it is quite safe to say, based on all of the evidence, that the American graphic quilts of the Baltimore style were the next step after the Medallion quilts. Medallion quilts were made primarily during the 18th century and I have not been able to find one that was made after 1820. Baltimore-style quilts were made from early in the 1800s through the

1870s. Almost all of the earliest Baltimore-style quilts have a large medallion-like center square, providing evidence of how the Medallion quilt became the Baltimore-style quilt. Picture 4 shows a southern appliqué quilt that is a Medallion quilt. The rows of designs and the center motif are all sewn to one large sheet of cloth. They are sewn in the rows so necessary to a Medallion quilt, but they are broken up into smaller units rather than being joined together. The next step was for the quilt makers to sew each of these broken motifs onto a square background block. The resulting quilt would definitely be an American graphic quilt. Oddly enough, about half of this quilt is cut chintz and half is regular appliqué cutout designs. This is an interesting quilt both for its historical value and for the intrinsic beauty of its design.

In one or two cases discussed in later chapters, the Midwestern style quilts will also be mentioned. As a regional style, this sort of quilt takes much from all of the eastern styles, so it is quite a mixture. Pieced quilts are more common than appliquéd ones. The NY-NJ style patterns were very popular, but the many colors used in a quilt top or even in a single block show a southern influence. The only truly Midwestern addition to quilt styling is the use of very little white. In the long winters, Midwesterners had only huge fields of white snow to look at, a view unbroken by the forests that covered the states east of the mountains. They did not want white, cold-looking quilts on their beds, too. Thus they made quilts with backgrounds of various colors, and even pastel shades were not used as widely as were darker colors.

To add to the material in this book, you may wish to look up other American graphic quilts illustrated in other quilt books. Do not look for them under the name American graphic quilts, but rather under the names in the small list of definitions in the front of this chapter. I believe that, as a group, these quilts deserve a name that they have never had before, so I coined the name American graphic for quilts made with blocks which differ in pattern on a single top. To find other examples, see the following:

American Quilts by Elizabeth W. Robertson. Studio Publications, 1948. This book has two 1815 quilts, one from the Brooklyn museum

Picture 2 Early Baltimore-style quilt owned by the Mount Vernon Ladies Association of the Union, Mount Vernon, Virginia.

Picture 3 A chintz quilt in block pattern. This is a southern quilt made in the 1850s, looted to the North during the Civil War. Courtesy Shelburne Museum, Shelburne, Vermont.

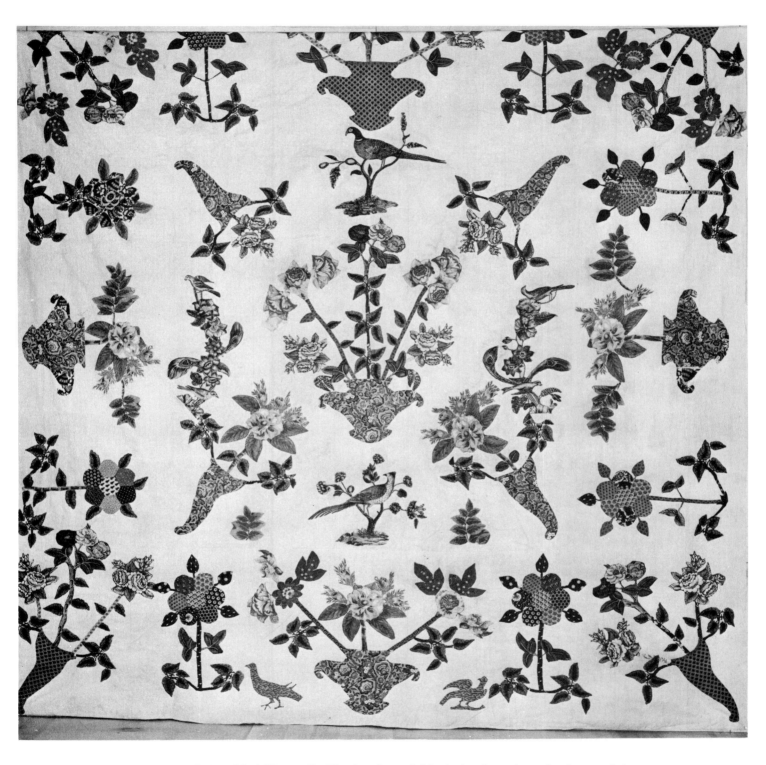

Picture 4   Chintz Medallion quilt. The borders of this design have been broken up into segments of the sort that, a little later, would be placed on blocks, the Baltimore-style quilt. Courtesy Shelburne Museum, Shelburne, Vermont.

and one which is a quilt listed as having been made in Baltimore, Maryland.

Quilts: Their Story and How to Make Them by Marie D. Webster. Gale Research Company, 1972. This book has a southern Indiana quilt of this type made in 1815.

The Romance of the Patchwork Quilt by Hall and Kretsinger. Caxton Printers, 1947. Two quilts of this type are shown.

Old Patchwork Quilts by Ruth E. Finley. Charles T. Bramford Company, 1971. Shows a remarkable quilt similar to quilts made after 1855 or in regions near the Ohio River at that time or even somewhat earlier.

These books are well known for their accuracy. There are several other books, both in and out of print, that have illustrations of American graphic quilts.

2

Foreign Influences

Some of the excitement of living in the seaport of Baltimore during the 1830s can be found in the quilts then made in that area. Motifs include not only the animals and flowers found in the householder's backyard, but also exotic animals and flowers seen only on imported cloth or china. The compositions are not only those taught by a girl's mother or neighborhood teacher, but also fancier ones copied from Dutch, Turkish, or Chinese models. There is a sophistication and verve about them that does not appear in the simpler quilts made in more rural areas.

The quilt in this chapter (Picture 5) is one of the oldest existing quilts of this kind. It clearly shows its Medallion quilt origins in the placement of the blocks. The second most noticeable feature of this quilt is the Oriental look of most of the motifs. In addition to the vase and its base in the center block, there are chrysanthemum-like forms in the flower shapes, an Oriental tree-like form in the grapevine in the second block from the top on the right-hand side, and a carp in the bottom block of the same row. The peacock and deer, Oriental motifs, were also used in European art. The foreign flavor of this quilt is illustrated by both Irish and Greek harps.

Through great good fortune, much is known about the life of Mrs. Rachel Meyer, the woman who made and designed this quilt, and in examining the quilt itself, more can be surmised about her. Mrs. Meyer was the daughter of German immigrants and may have been an immigrant herself. She met and married her husband in Baltimore, where her nine children (eight sons and one daughter) were born. According to family records, she was born in 1818 and died in 1867. During most of her life, she was devoted to fine needlework as a leisure time activity. She left several pieces of her work, among which are the two quilts illustrated in the second and third chapters of this book.

Mrs. Meyer made this quilt of home-dyed, homespun materials. The only material in this quilt that was bought was the red fabric (which could not be produced from the vegetable dyes available at that time) and a small piece of black velvet. These two pieces of cloth had to be imported. The red cloth was not as sturdy as the homespun cloth used in the remainder of the quilt and it is much mended. I wish I knew where Mrs. Meyer got the piece of velvet and why she treasured it enough to fit it into her quilt. There are several shades of blue in the quilt. This suggests either cloth from an uneven dyeing, or the results of several dyeings, in which case the blues were scraps left over from clothing.

A soft salmon color, rather faded, was probably an attempt at making red cloth with Mrs. Meyer's vegetable dyes. It was first used for lattice strips between the blocks, but shortly after the quilt was finished, this salmon-colored cloth was used to patch the red cloth. This first patching of the red cloth with the salmon cloth was obviously done by Mrs. Meyer, since she carefully clipped the stitches of the overlapping pieces and slipped the salmon cloth underneath. The patching was then buttonholed down. This sort of mending was not continued and the later patching does not show the neatness of the first. The stitches also change, showing that the later patching was done by another owner.

The background material of the quilt is bleached, white homespun material. The backing and several motifs are also made of this white homespun. The leaves and stems are green with a pronounced yellowish tone and a greenish-yellow color is also used extensively. Both of the colors were obviously obtained from vegetable dyes. Other colors are tan, two small pieces of the famous butternut brown, and a grayish-white, not of the same material as the background but still homespun.

Picture 5 Early Baltimore-style quilt, the first Rachel Meyer quilt, showing Medallion quilt characteristics. By permission of Mrs. Alice F. Hecht, owner.

12

In all, the stitches of three persons appear on this quilt. First, there are Mrs. Meyer's stitches. In the center block, two buds and a leaf are in a child's stitches, rather uneven but as small as possible. The third person who worked on the quilt made the later stitches on the patches and they are not as neat and tiny as those of Mrs. Meyer or as careful as those of the child.

We will discuss the motifs later in this chapter but first I would like to refer you to the two figures on horseback (*See* Figures 3 and 4). These figures were copies from popular engravings of the day and represent the American heroes General Andrew Jackson (on the left) and President George Washington (on the right). This is a posthumous tribute to Washington, who died in 1799. The figure of General Jackson, however, tells us something about Mrs. Meyer and helps to date the quilt. The first public notice taken of General Jackson was when the forces under him defeated the Creek Indians at Horseshoe Bend, Alabama, in 1814. This skirmish took place during the War of 1812 at a time when the British were encouraging the Indians to make war on the frontiers. He then went into the Territory of Florida and won a victory against the British troops stationed at Pensacola. He then moved on to New Orleans and on January 8, 1815, his men won a rousing victory over the previously invincible British. The victory won undying fame for Jackson throughout the eighteen United States, but the date is still too early for this quilt.

General Jackson went on to win other battles against the Indians and became the first Governor of Florida after it entered the Union in 1819. His service had made him one of the most famous men of his time and to the frontiersmen and eastern farmers he was a great hero, second only to Washington. He was proposed for President in 1822 and formally nominated as a candidate in 1824. He lost this election because of a technicality. He was then sent to Washington, D.C., as a senator from Tennessee and served for about one year before resigning to devote his time to a second Presidential campaign. This campaign was successful, and he was elected President in 1828. His term lasted from 1829 until 1837, and I believe that Mrs. Meyer made her quilt between these years. In fact, the figure may have been taken from campaign posters from the election campaign in 1833 when President Jackson was elected to a

second term. This date falls in the mid-point of the years when Yankee clipper ships were bringing Chinese exports into our eastern ports, which is consistent with the Chinese motifs dominating this quilt.

Figure 5 shows the center block of Mrs. Meyer's quilt and Figure 6 shows an extremely similar block in a wool embroidered rug made by ten-year-old Jane Grove of Wiscasset, Maine, in 1845. Jane embroidered her designs in wool on wool and this explains the cruder figures and flowers. The similarities in the figures, vase, and flowers, and their placement on the block are too great to be coincidental. The design probably appeared in a book used for inspiration by both Mrs. Meyer and Jane Grove. Jane's rug is now in California at the Museum of the City of Los Angeles.

General Jackson, shouting "Charge!" while astride his spirited tan charger, is graphically pictured in Figure 3 just as Mrs. Meyer appliquéd him when the quilt was new. The loss of his boot and a piece of his horse's tail detract nothing from this design. Mrs. Meyer loved to embroider small details with short stitches of embroidery and although many stitches have worn away with time, enough remains to tell us of the painstaking labor she did. These stitches, in rows of red and white, are used for the General's plume in his brown hat. In brown, they form his hair; in black, his eyes and eyebrows; and in red, his mouth. In red, they provide the horse with reins and in brown they create its hooves. Rows of white stitches give the General his epaulets. His sword decoration and tassel are in pink wool. Buttonhole stitches of pink wool, every bit as tiny as the other embroidery, finish off his saddle blanket. The General's face and hands and the horse's eyes are white. The General's coat and saddle blanket are red, while his trousers are blue. The saddle, shown between his hand and trousers, is tan, as is his sword. The embroidery that is not wool is single strand silk thread.

Poor General Washington has lost his trousers as well as his boots, but he tips his hat as politely as he ever did. The General rides a white horse with tan reins and a red saddle blanket. He wears a brown hat, black velvet shirt, tan waistcoat, and a blue coat with tan facings. Mrs. Meyer's embroidery stitches form a red cockade in his hat, brown hair, a black eye, and white epaulets. In tan, they form the horse's mane, tail, and hooves. In brown, they form the

Figure 3 General Jackson in appliqué from the first Rachel Meyer quilt.

Figure 4 General Washington in appliqué from the first Rachel Meyer quilt.

Figure 5 Center block from the first Rachel Meyer quilt, made in the 1830s in Baltimore, Maryland.

Figure 6 Center motif of the 1840 Jane Grove wool rug from Wiscasset, Maine.

16

horse's eye and part of the reins. Gold thread was used to buttonhole the saddle blanket and a white wool daisy stitch forms a further trim.

These two figures resemble other representations in engravings and woodcuts of the day so closely that even though I could not find the exact pictures they were copied from, we may be sure of their identity. In the illustrations that follow, I have tried to show articles that would have been available to Mrs. Meyer as material to copy in her quilt. That she copied patterns from many other craft patterns cannot be denied. However, the way she combined these patterns to form the designs of her quilt is unique and beautiful.

In her work, Mrs. Meyer used several vases, which might at first glance seem to be originals. These are shown in Figures 7, 9, and 10. Figure 8 is a Japanese-made shaving bowl brought to this country at about the same time that Mrs. Meyer was making her quilt. Although she could not have seen this particular bowl except by a great coincidence, she could have seen other dishes of this sort, and it certainly resembles the vase in the center block of her quilt. I could not find other near matches in the material available, but I have included two Delft tiles (Figures 11 and 12) showing the fanciful vases that were used in the art of that day.

The vase in Figure 7 is made from yellow cloth edged with red embroidery and trimmed at the center with white embroidery. In Figure 9, the vase is yellow with a red center and brown embroidery. The vase in Figure 10 has a yellow center with five red slits, while the top and bottom of the vase are white and the embroidery is pink. The vase in Figure 13 is tan with a red shape in approximately the middle and is trimmed with yellow embroidery. Figure 14 is blue in the center with white slits and a yellow top and bottom. There is no embroidery on this motif. Figure 15, which may not be a vase since a cat is appliquéd to it in the block, is blue with pink embroidery. Figure 16 is blue in the center with yellow slits and a red top and bottom, while the embroidery is yellow. Figure 17 has a white center, blue top, and red bottom, and the embroidery is again yellow. Figure 18, which also may or may not be a vase, is blue without any embroidery.

In these vases, Mrs. Meyer placed a remarkable assembly of flowers and fruits. Figures 19 through 23 show her rose-like flowers. In Figure 24, I have sketched a rose painted by one of the itinerant limners of the American Primitive tradition. The white object in the sketch is the hand of the child shown in the painting. Except for the second rose (Figure 20), these flowers resemble the traditional quilter's rose, although they are a little more elaborate than most. Figure 19 is, from the center out, tan, white, red, tan, blue, and tan. Figure 20 is yellow, light red, and dark red. Figure 21 is yellow, red, tan, and blue. Figure 22 has a blue center embroidered with pink wool and four rows of white petals. Figure 23 has a yellow center with white embroidery and then rows of red, white, red, white, and blue petals. These roses show how versatile Mrs. Meyer's imagination was.

Figures 25 through 29 show the tulip motifs Mrs. Meyer used.

Figure 25 is blue with a white top and brown embroidery. Figure 26 is, from the center out, white, blue, and red. Figure 27 is red with yellow slits. Figure 28 is, from the bottom up, yellow, red, and grayish-white. Figure 29 is red and white. Figure 30 shows the front board from a carved and painted chest made in Connecticut. These tulips are also similar to, but more elaborate than, the quilter's traditional tulip.

Figures 31 through 36 show Mrs. Meyer's peony-like flowers. These flowers were also quite popular on the Chinese export china that was arriving on the China clipper ships. Figure 31 is blue. Figure 32 is, from the bottom up, yellow and red, and has a green leaf at the top. Figure 33 is yellow with brown embroidery. Figure 34 is yellow and red, while Figure 35 is also yellow and red with white dots in the center and dark brown embroidery. Figure 36 is, from the bottom, yellow, red, yellow, white, dark blue, and light blue.

Figures 37 through 40 show some of the flowers in Mrs. Meyer's quilt that I am unable to classify. There are many of these flower types in early quilting and they were surely taken from the Jacobean-style embroidery called crewelwork. These flowers were designed from real flowers viewed from above, below, cut in half, sideways, and from many other positions. Figure 41 shows a crewelwork flower that resembles the quilted flower in Figure 40. Figure 37 has two green leaves at the bottom, a tan center, and two red petals, while the main body of the flower is blue. Figure 38 has three sets of green leaves each

Figure 7 Vase from center block of the first Rachel Meyer quilt.

Figure 8 Imari-style shaving bowl.

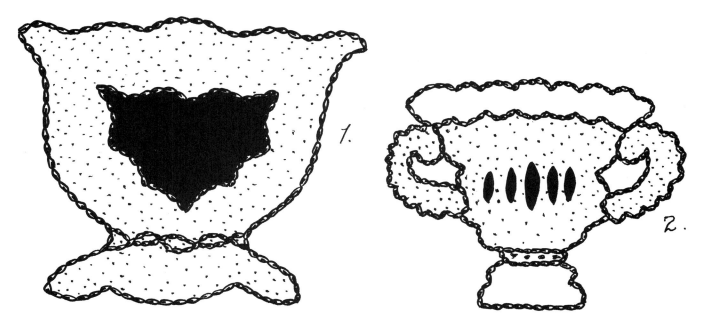

Figures 9 and 10 Vases from the first Rachel Meyer quilt.

Figures 11 and 12 Two Delft tiles from a set for a fireplace.

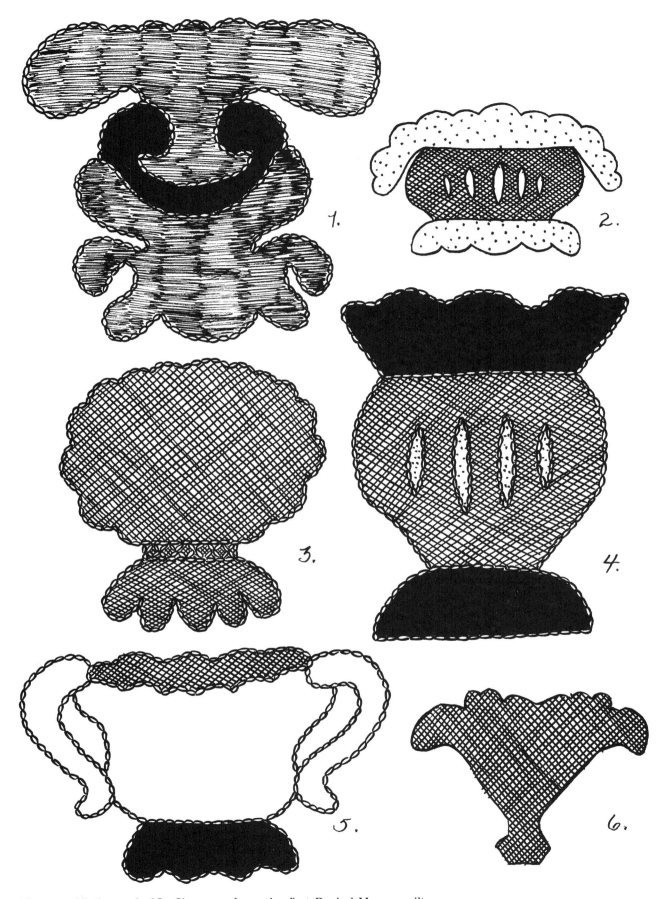

Figures 13 through 18 Six vases from the first Rachel Meyer quilt.

20

Figures 19 through 23 Five roses from the first Rachel Meyer quilt.

Figure 24 Rose in American Primitive portrait.

21

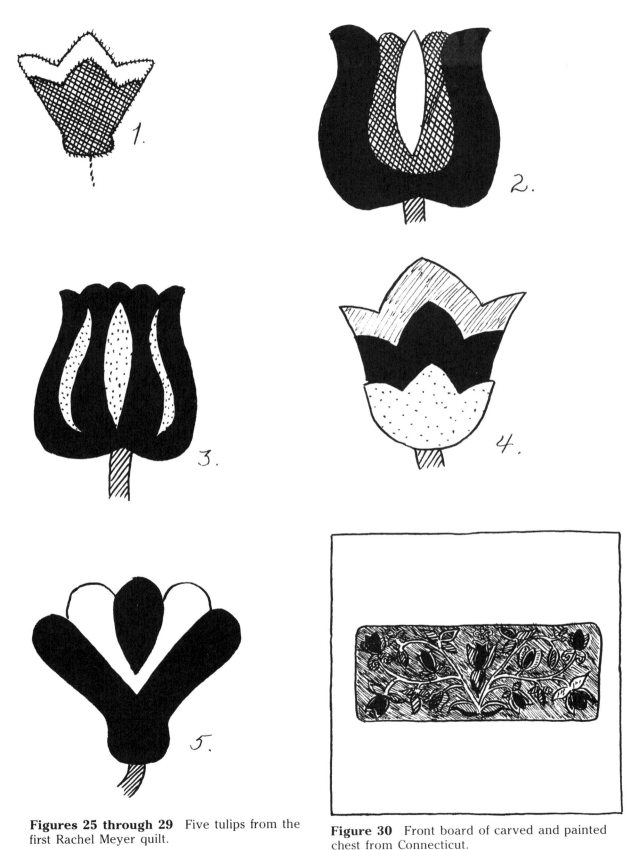

Figures 25 through 29 Five tulips from the first Rachel Meyer quilt.

Figure 30 Front board of carved and painted chest from Connecticut.

Figures 31 through 36 Six peony-like flowers from the first Rachel Meyer quilt.

1.

2.

3.

Figures 37 through 40 Four odd flowers from the first Rachel Meyer quilt.

4.

Figure 41 Crewelwork design.

24

on the outside, red dots on a yellow background, and a circle of tan embroidery outlining it. Figure 39 is blue with white slits, and Figure 40 has yellow and red petals inside a tan ring surrounded by green petals.

Figures 42 through 56 also show designed flower forms. Figure 42 is tan and blue with yellow embroidery; Figure 43 is, from the center out, white, red, and yellow; Figure 44 has a green bottom, tan center, white, with three yellow and two green dots on a red background; the tan center section is embroidered in pink thread. Figure 45 is blue and yellow; Figures 46 and 49 are yellow bud-like forms on green, and each has embroidery outlines in brown thread. Figure 47 is tan with brown embroidery. Figure 48 is blue with yellow embroidery on both the large form and on the two buds. The bases are green. Figures 50 through 52 show some really bizarre flowers. Figure 50 is red on yellow. Figure 51 has blue petals at the bottom with two green leaves rising out of either side and a red top with yellow slits. Figure 52 has a green base, red on yellow center, and red on green buds at the top. Figure 53 has a bud-like cluster flower form with white flowers and green bases, and yellow stems rising out of the center green stem. Figure 54 is yellow on a green base with yellow embroidery. Figure 55 has tan petals on a green base and yellow embroidery. Figure 56 has a white petal at the base, two red petals above that, and a yellow petal on a green base above those. The embroidery is brown with pink circles at the ends of the stamen.

To further show where Mrs. Meyer may have found the inspiration for her odd flowers, Figure 57 is a section of a painted cotton hanging from India. Figure 58 is a motif from English Delft china, and Figure 59 is a section of French Mock India wallpaper. Figure 60 shows a page of illuminated Fraktur from a Pennsylvania-made prayer book. The art of illustrating books with Fraktur work grew out of the Medieval illuminated religious volumes made in European monasteries.

The buds of these flowers show the excellence of Mrs. Meyer's inventiveness. There are fifteen different forms, each quite different from the last. The first bud, Figure 61, is all red with a brown embroidered stem. Figure 62 is a red bud on a green base, again with an embroidered stem. Figure 63 is yellow with red slits and an embroidered stem.

Figure 64 is red on green with brown embroidery. Figure 65 is yellow with blue and brown embroidery. Figure 66 is white with red slits on a green base. Figures 67 and 68 are white on green with the same brown stems as most of the others. Figure 69 is yellow with a red slit and a green base. Figures 70 and 71 are red with green bases. Figure 72 is white on green, and Figure 73 is blue with brown embroidery. Figure 74 is white and red, and Figure 75 is tan and red on green. Figure 72 has a green stem rather than the embroidered stems of the other forms.

If you think Mrs. Meyer used all of her inventiveness on the flowers and buds, just look at the leaves shown in Figures 76 through 91. These are all done in varying shades of green, but the forms and trims make each quite individual. Figure 77 has red embroidery; Figure 78 has a white stripe and brown embroidery; Figure 79 has white embroidery; and Figure 80 has brown embroidery. Figures 81 and 87 repeat the white embroidery; Figures 82 and 86 have yellow ribs, with 86 having the darker color; Figures 88 and 89 each have a red embroidered rib. The others (Figures 76, 83, 84, 85, 90, and 91) are plain green without trim.

The quilt is aflutter with ten different birds, some flying and some perching on the branches. The two birds shown in Figures 92 and 93 are obviously of the same kind, but I could not identify them until I found a painting on the beam of a barn, done by an itinerant barn painter during the last century (See Figure 94). It now seems that these birds are American passenger pigeons, now extinct and unfamiliar to modern eyes but quite familiar to people in Mrs. Meyer's era when great flocks still darkened the sky during migration. There is nothing that dates the quilt as a very early one more than this casual inclusion of a bird now lost forever. The pigeons are done in tan and blue and yellow and blue.

Mrs. Meyer may have had a specific bird species in mind when she cut out and appliquéd the birds shown in Figures 95 through 99. Except for Figure 98, which suggests a Carolina parakeet, and Figure 99, which may have been meant to be a mockingbird, these are very unlikely birds indeed. Figure 95 is yellow with a blue wing, a white eye, and pink embroidery on its neck and feet. Figure 96 shows a small white bird with green wings and pink embroidery. Figure 97 is a tan bird with a white eye.

Figures 42 through 44 Three odd flowers from the first Rachel Meyer quilt.

Figures 45 through 49 Five flowers from the first Rachel Meyer quilt.

Figures 50 through 52   Three flowers from the first Rachel Meyer quilt.

28

Figures 53 through 56 Four flowers from the first Rachel Meyer quilt.

Figure 57 Design from painted cotton hanging from India.

Figure 58 Design from English Delft china.

Figure 59 Section of French Mock India wallpaper.

Figure 60 Illuminated Fraktur from page in Pennsylvania prayer book.

Figures 61 through 75 Fifteen flower buds from the first Rachel Meyer quilt.

Figures 76 through 91 Sixteen leaves from the first Rachel Meyer quilt.

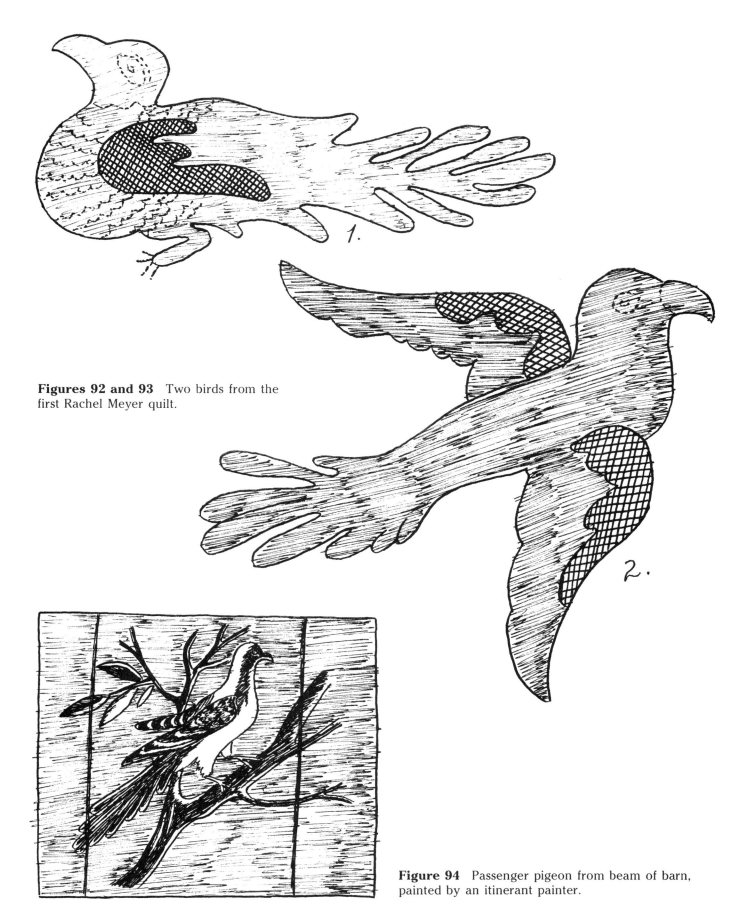

Figures 92 and 93 Two birds from the first Rachel Meyer quilt.

Figure 94 Passenger pigeon from beam of barn, painted by an itinerant painter.

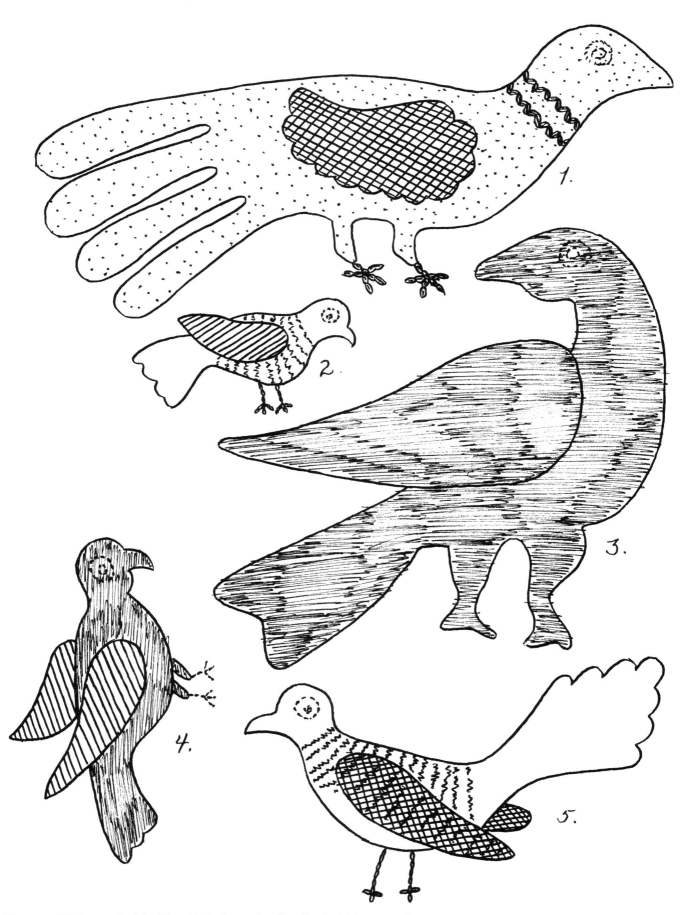

Figures 95 through 99 Five birds from the first Rachel Meyer quilt.

The parakeet-like bird in Figure 98 is white with blue wings and pink embroidery. The mockingbird in Figure 99 is white with blue wings and pink embroidery, and the legs are embroidered in brown.

The birds in Figures 100 through 102 are quite clear. They are an eagle, a dove, and a peacock. The eagle, of course, represents the United States. The dove with the heart represents peace and love, then as now, but did have another meaning at that time — it represented women. A party given by and for women is now called a "hen party," but in the early years of the 18th century it would have been called a "dove party." The peacock may have been included because of its symbolical meanings of avariciousness or majesty or because Mrs. Meyer had seen peacocks and thought them pretty. The design is real enough to make me think that Mrs. Meyer had really seen one, a supposition that is not as far-fetched as it might seem at first; wealthy people were known to have had these birds on their estates during colonial times.

From this era, I have included sketches of a carved eagle headboard (*See* Figure 103), and an odd tin bird-shaped cookie cutter (*See* Figure 104). The eagle (*See* Figure 100) is white with white embroidery and

Figures 100 through 102   Three birds from the first Rachel Meyer quilt.

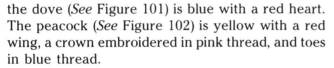

Figure 103 Carved eagle headboard on 1815 bed.

Figure 104 Tin cookie cutter.

the dove (*See* Figure 101) is blue with a red heart. The peacock (*See* Figure 102) is yellow with a red wing, a crown embroidered in pink thread, and toes in blue thread.

I do not know how many children Mrs. Meyer had when she made this quilt, but she must have had at least one because she allowed a child to appliqué a leaf and two buds in the center section of the middle block. That she had children is also evident in the animals appearing on the quilt, which are added in a way that would be sure to delight young children. The family cat and the family horse are shown. Deer and squirrel are pictured for the hunters in the family, and the fish is for the fishermen. All of these animals were used in other art forms of the time. Horses were popular in paintings and etchings. They were frequently used on tavern and shop signs and some towns were even named after taverns with famous horse signs. If you look on a map at the eastern border of Pennsylvania along U.S. 1, you will find a small town called "White Horse." A famous stagecoach stop and tavern was situated there from earliest colonial times. Its sign was a painted white horse which was a welcome sight to travelers going from Philadelphia to Baltimore.

The horse on this quilt (*See* Figure 105) is particularly well-executed, with shapely legs and a good head, unlike the shapes of some of the other animal motifs.

He is bright red with a yellow strap around his middle and a white strap around his neck. His harness is yellow and the reins are brown embroidery. His mane and tail are white stitches, his hooves are brown stitches, and his eye is white with a brown center.

Figure 106 shows one of the two deer and Figure 107 shows the squirrel from the quilt. Figures 108 and 109 show two chalk or plaster of paris figures which were sold door-to-door by itinerant peddlers and were very popular for many years in the 18th and 19th centuries. It may have been from figures like these that Mrs. Meyer obtained the outlines for some of the figures on her quilt. The deer in Figure 106 is white with brown embroidered antlers and hooves and pink embroidered eyes. The squirrel in Figure 107 is yellow with white embroidered eyes, and is holding a green embroidered nut.

The last three animals are a carp (Figure 110), a cat (Figure 111), and a stag (Figure 112). The carp looks very much like those drawn on Chinese export china. Carp were considered a wish for long life and good fortune by the artists who drew them. This carp is red with a white eye and blue center. The body of this fish must have been covered with the outlines of scales done in Mrs. Meyer's tiny stitches, but most of them have worn off, leaving only a few white lines hinting at where she originally placed

Figure 105 Horse from the first Rachel Meyer quilt.

them. The cat is yellow with yellow embroidery, and the stag is tan with light red antlers, pink and brown embroidered eyes, and brown embroidered hooves.

Mrs. Meyer put four butterflies in her garden. Butterflies were quite popular motifs on cloth. They were painted, printed, and embroidered on many kinds of wearing apparel and household linens. Figure 113 shows a part of the design of an English printed cotton of that period. The first butterfly (*See* Figure 114) has a red body, blue upper wings, and white lower wings with a fancy pattern embroidered in brown on them. Figure 115 is tan with blue wings and reddish embroidery. Figure 116 is white with yellow wings, and there is very little remaining of the brown

embroidered pattern on its wings. The last butterfly (Figure 117) has a blue body, red upper wings, and white lower wings with brown embroidery.

Fruit motifs were used extensively on furniture made in the 1840s. In fact, so much fruit was carved or painted on this furniture that it is one of the features sought when dating furniture. It is not surprising that Mrs. Meyer used fruit when it was becoming so popular. The quilt includes a whole wreath of strawberries, which are the ripest, most luscious-looking fruit imaginable. She also used pears, cherries, and what must be plums. A bunch of grapes is inserted in the center bouquet and is the sort of thing that needlewomen did in those days. I found a period

Figures 106 and 107 Deer and squirrel from the first Rachel Meyer quilt.

Figure 108 Chalk figure of deer.

Figure 109 Chalk figure of squirrel.

Figures 110 through 112 Three animals from the first Rachel Meyer quilt.

39

Figure 113 Design from English printed cotton — 1830.

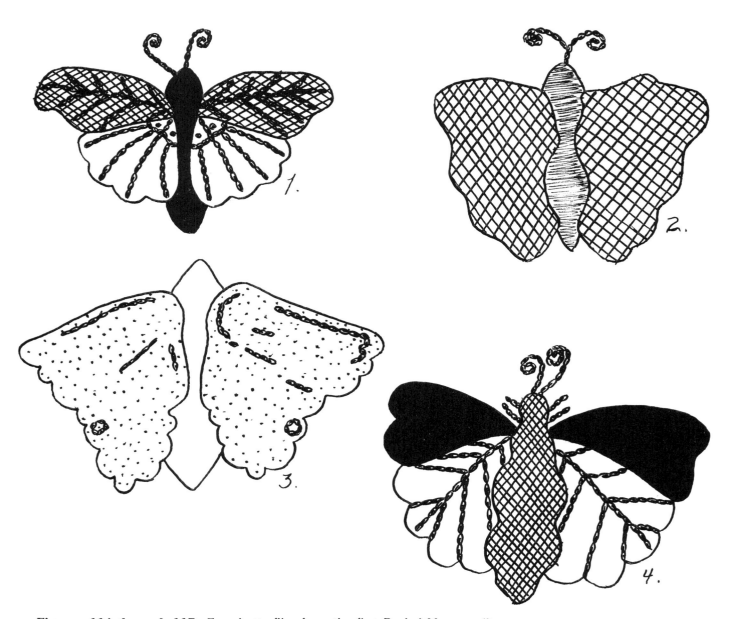

Figures 114 through 117 Four butterflies from the first Rachel Meyer quilt.

40

clock with a painted glass panel which had a fine group of fruit. This clock has always belonged to a Virginia family named Bowie. The present owners have given me permission to copy it (*See* Figure 118). Fruit designs were also used on shop signs, in primitive paintings, on Hitchcock chairs, and on many other objects which Mrs. Meyer could have seen and copied. The pears (*See* Figure 119) are red and yellow, and grayish-white and green on a green stem which has two green leaves. The leaves have white embroidered veins. The grapes (*See* Figure 120) in the center block are white with a green stem and red embroidered curlicues. The five bunches of grapes in the grapevine block are white, blue, red, blue, and white from right to left. The cherries (*See* Figure 121) are both red and yellow on a green stem with two leaves. These leaves also have white embroidered veins. The plums (*See* Figure 122) are blue and yellow or green and yellow on a green stem with a green leaf. This is a most elaborate leaf and has the usual white veins. The strawberries (*See* Figure 123) are red on a green base with yellow dots of embroidery for seeds and brown embroidered stems.

Figures 124 through 129 show several of the incidental motifs which Mrs. Meyer used to fill in odd corners of her quilt. The two harps mentioned before appear in Figures 124 and 125 and are both red, although the Greek harp (*See* Figure 124) has yellow embroidery. The Greek harp was a favorite motif of

Empire period designers, and therefore had to be quite familiar to Mrs. Meyer. I was quite puzzled by the Irish harp (knowing Mrs. Meyer's German background), but then I found a picture of a chair whose back included a similar motif. Two chairs showing the two harps are shown in Figures 126 and 127. The cannon (*See* Figure 128), which appears with the figure of General Jackson, must originally have come from the same drawing as the portrait. Most of the embroidery has worn off the white flag, so we cannot know what device it carried, but it could not have been a flag of surrender. The carriage is tan, the barrel is blue, and the wheel rim is white. The embroidery is used on the outside of the wheel and for the flag staff. What little embroidery is left on the flag is also tan. The wheel spokes are red embroidery and that on the cannon barrel is pink. The motif in Figure 129 is an enigma. It looks like an ice-cream sundae, complete with a cherry on top, but since the sundae had not been invented yet, and even ice cream was quite rare, I think my guess must be wrong. One of these strange motifs is red with yellow embroidery and the other is yellow with red embroidery. They are probably architectural motifs but why they are where they are in the quilt is anybody's guess.

Scrolls were frequently used in Empire furniture, as shown by the chair in Figure 130. Mrs. Meyer used quite graceful scrolls. Figures 131, 132, and 135 are red, Figure 133 is green, and Figure 134 is yellow.

I have purposely broken up the block motifs in this chapter to show you where the different motifs could have been obtained. Now try to identify the different motifs in the drawing of the quilt top (*See* Picture 5). In doing this, you will begin to realize how very skillfully Mrs. Meyer combined these odd elements into a pleasing whole. This quilt is impressive in that so many different and difficult elements were carefully planned beforehand so that each fits into its place in the design without any overlapping or compromising, unlike most quilts of this period. This is most noticeable in the border (*See* Figure 136), where each side and corner is exactly like the others. The corners are turned well and the vine fits this turn perfectly. Almost none of the quilts made in the first half of the 19th century have corners that are even similar to one another, since each was turned as the quilter came to it, which entailed fitting the design and cutting the corner as necessary.

Figure 118 Clock with painted glass panel showing fruit — 1834.

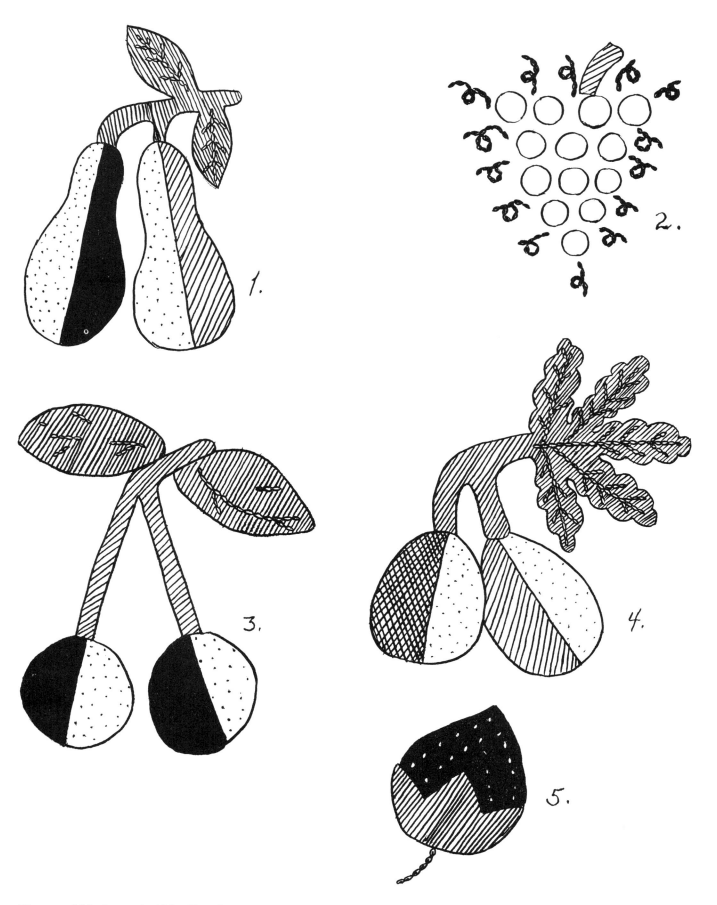

Figures 119 through 123   Five fruit designs from the first Rachel Meyer quilt.

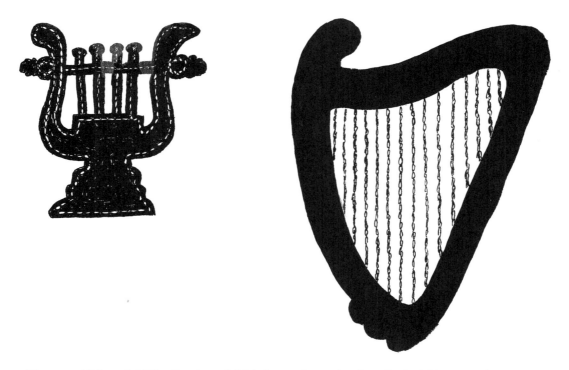

Figures 124 and 125 Greek and Irish harps from the first Rachel Meyer quilt.

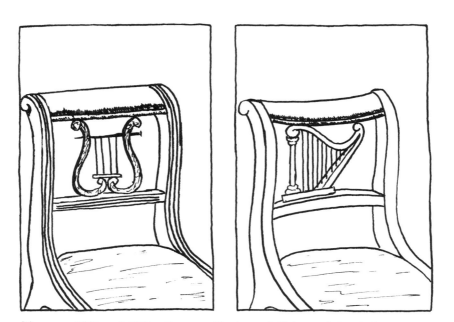

Figures 126 and 127 Duncan Phyfe and Chippendale chairs.

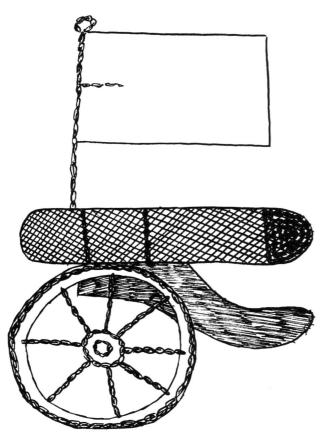

Figure 128 Cannon from the first Rachel Meyer quilt.

Figure 129 Unidentified motif from the first Rachel Meyer quilt.

Figure 130 Chair from Annapolis, Maryland — 1830-1835.

The border (*See* Figure 136) is composed of a flower vine, the flowers of which are unlike those on the rest of the quilt. However, because the scale and materials are the same as those used in the rest of the quilt, the border fits in with the design.

This quilt tells us other things about Mrs. Meyer— her personality and her circumstances. Mrs. Meyer was a well-trained seamstress. She was quite artistic and loved beautiful things, or she would never have taken the time and effort required to finish this quilt. She seems to have loved children because she used motifs that children would like and because she allowed a child to do some sewing on this master-piece of a quilt. Politically, she must have been a Democrat, since the Jackson motif was used when this was a political, not a historical, design. Mrs. Meyer must have been poor when she made this quilt, because the materials used were mostly those she could produce by her own work rather than those she had to buy. The cloth is homespun and the filler is hand-carded cotton, used when print material and ginned cotton were available. No frame was used when this quilt was quilted, indicating either poverty or a very small house. Quilts done on a quilting frame are quite easily distinguished from those done otherwise. Mrs. Meyer also apparently was interested in new things and ways. Chinese objects were just beginning to come into this country, and the motifs on this quilt were not copied from secondhand designs on European imports, which had been available for some time, but were obviously

Figures 131 through 135 Five scrolls from the first Rachel Meyer quilt.

Picture 5 First Rachel Meyer quilt.

46

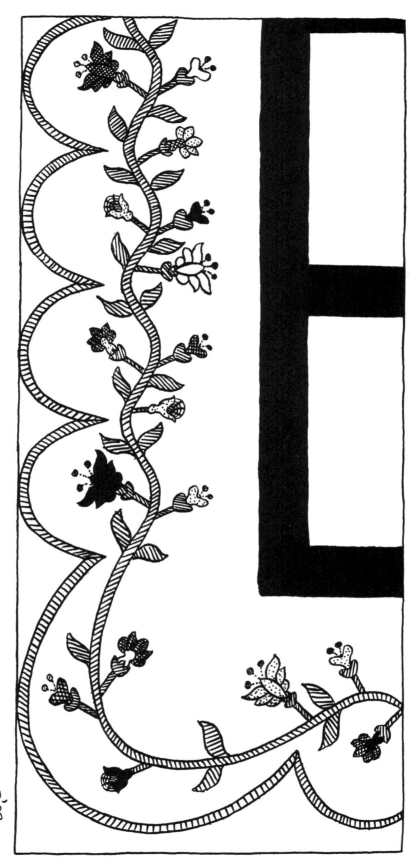

Figure 136 Border and corner on the first Rachel Meyer quilt.

copied from Oriental originals. Only a flexible personality can take a new art form and use it successfully in one's own designs.

The quilt now belongs to a descendant of Mrs. Meyer, who lives in Baltimore just as her ancestor did. This circumstance has allowed the quilt and its history to come down to us intact. It is a most beautiful and interesting example of an early American graphic quilt of the Baltimore style.

On the following pages, you will find exact-size patterns for the first Rachel Meyer quilt. The center block is 38 inches square, the smaller squares are 18 inches on a side, and the latticed strips are two inches wide. The patterns are drawn to finished size, which means that one-fourth-inch seam allowances must be left on all sides of all patterns, background squares, lattice strips, and border strips. Refer to the preceding text for the colors used in each motif.

The total depth of the border is eleven inches. To make the outer edge of the border, cut a pattern for the center scallops and draw these along the outer edge of the border. To make the round corners, cut a circle eleven inches in diameter. Draw the outline of the circle on the corner of the border strip and extend the ends of the scroll to meet the circle. Study the outline of the quilt border edge carefully as you read these directions. When the border edge has been drawn, place the appliqué vine so that the lowest points are opposite the top of the scallops, as the finished drawing shows.

The flowers should be red, tan, white, yellow, light blue, and dark blue. Mix the flowers and do not make adjoining flowers the same color. The binding on the edge of the finished quilt should be green.

The quilting on this quilt should be outline, with simple diagonal line fill-in for the background.

Center block (block 1) from first Rachel Meyer quilt.

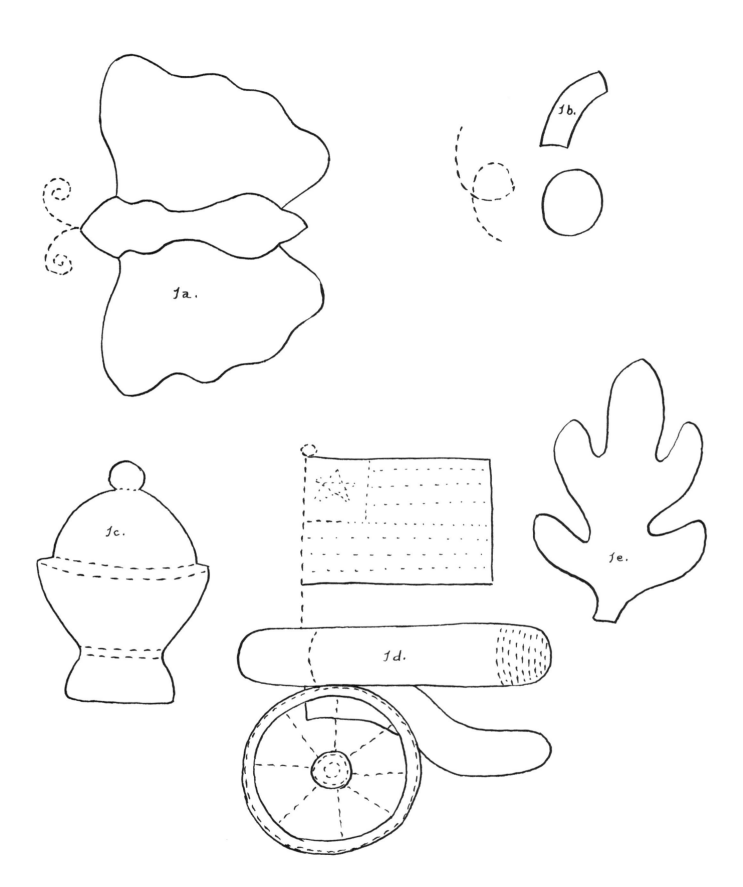

1a.

1b.

1c.

1d.

1e.

49

1f.

1g.

1h.

1j.

1k.

1L.

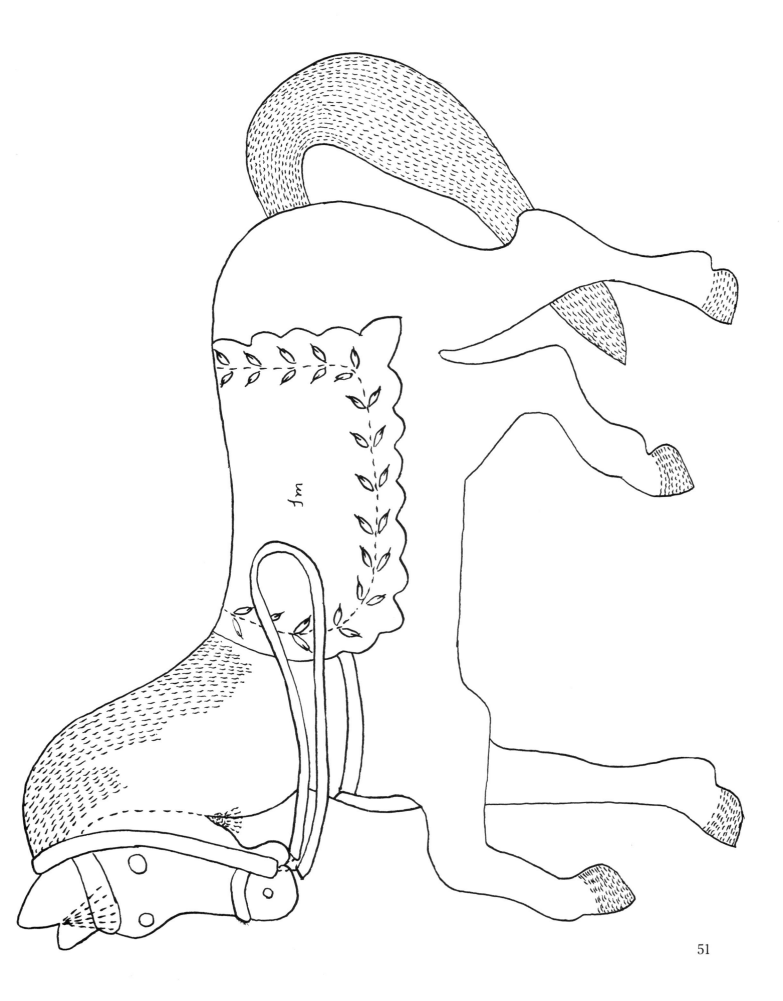

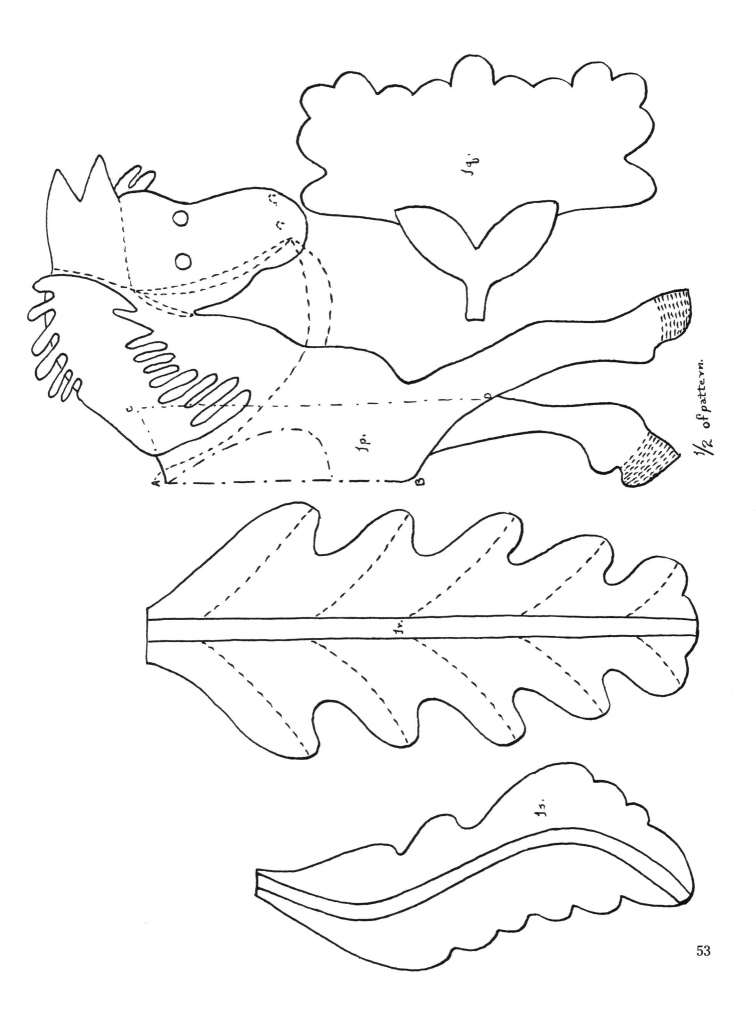

½ of pattern.

53

½ of pattern

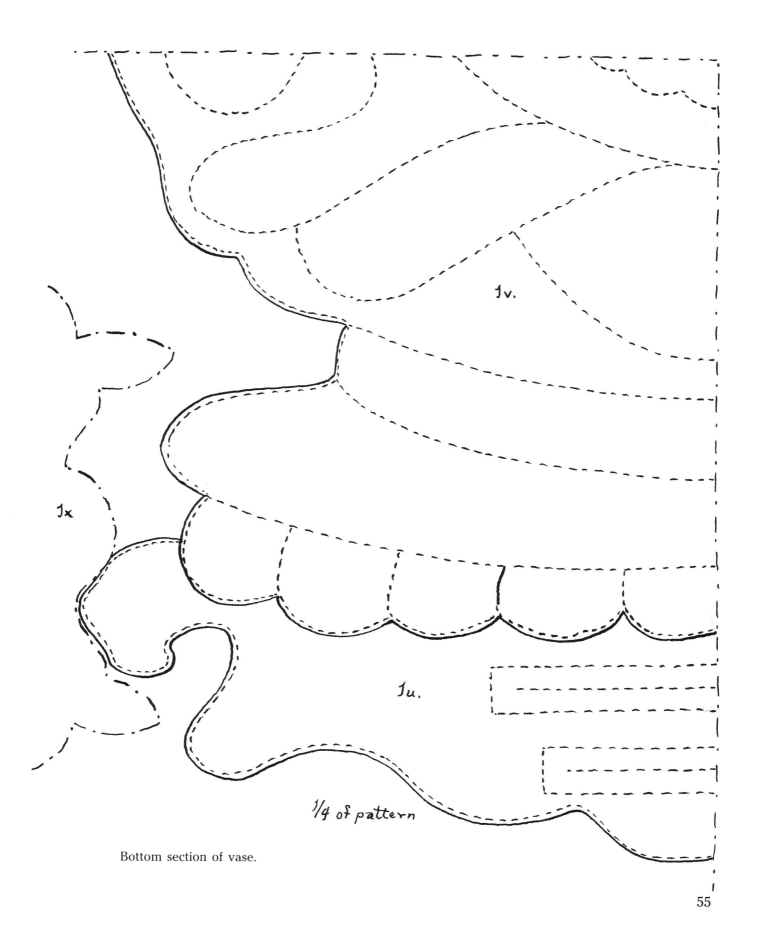

1v.

1x

1u.

¼ of pattern

Bottom section of vase.

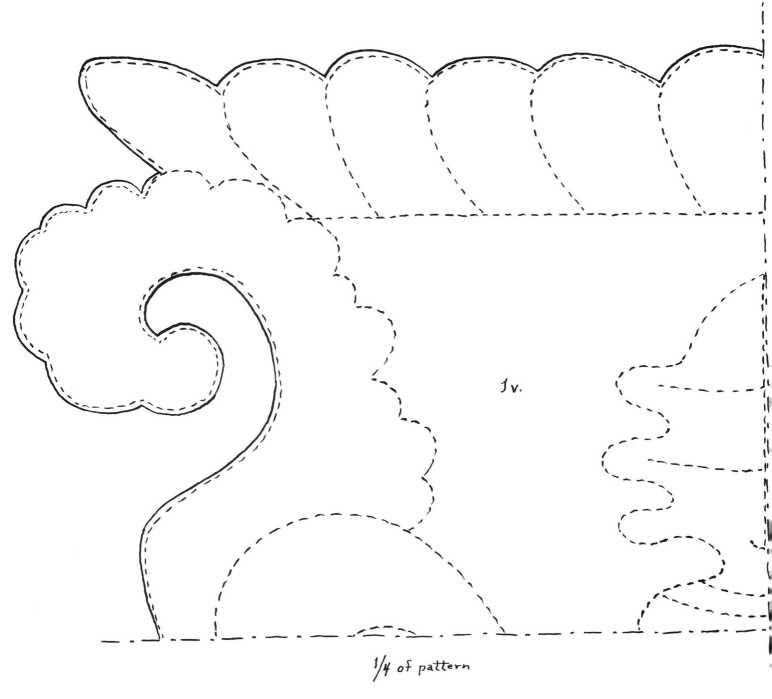

1/4 of pattern

1 v.

Top section of vase.

Scrolls near bottom of vase.

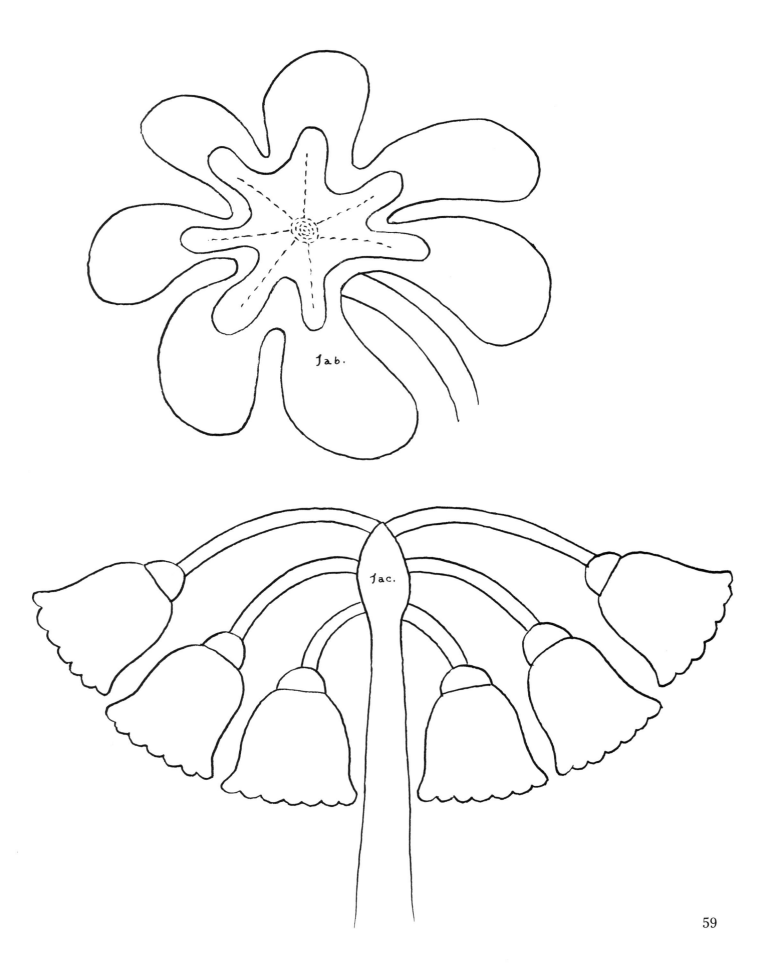

59

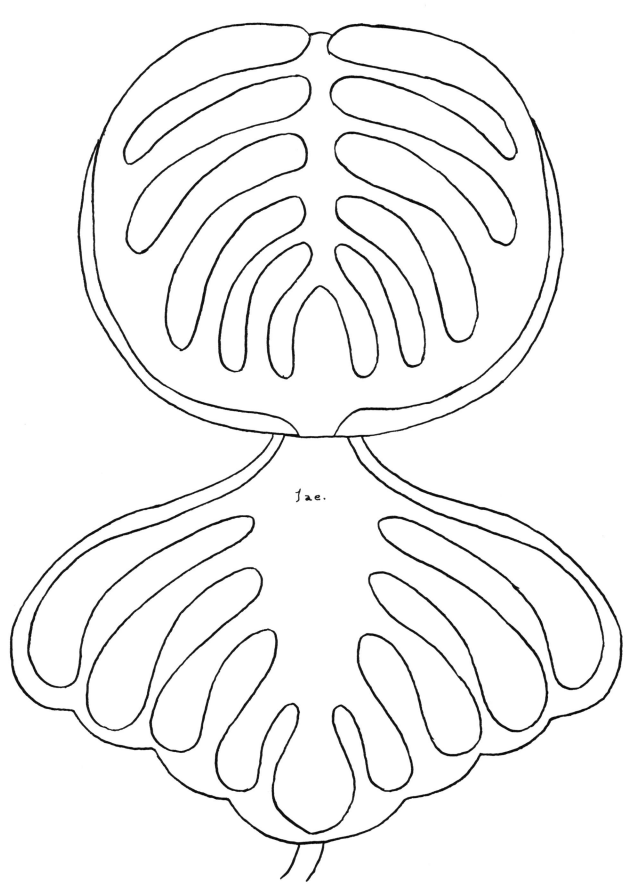

fae.

61

62

Jag.

Jah.

2

2a

2b.

2c.

2d.

2e.

2f.

Block 2 from the first Rachel Meyer quilt.

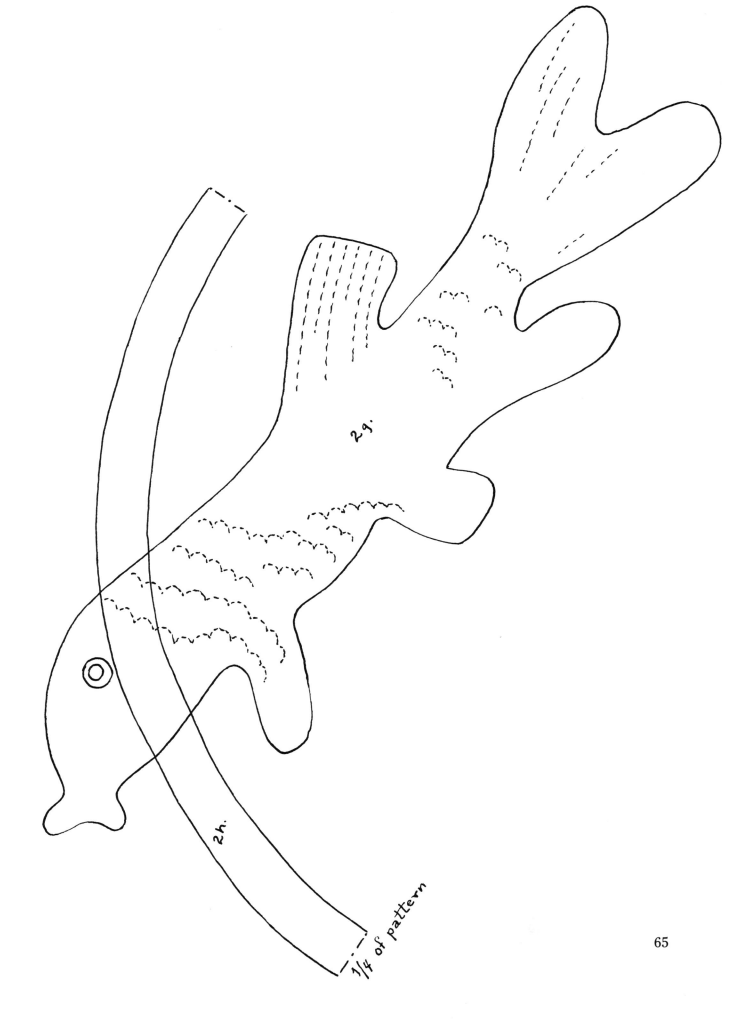

2g.

2h.

1/4 of pattern

65

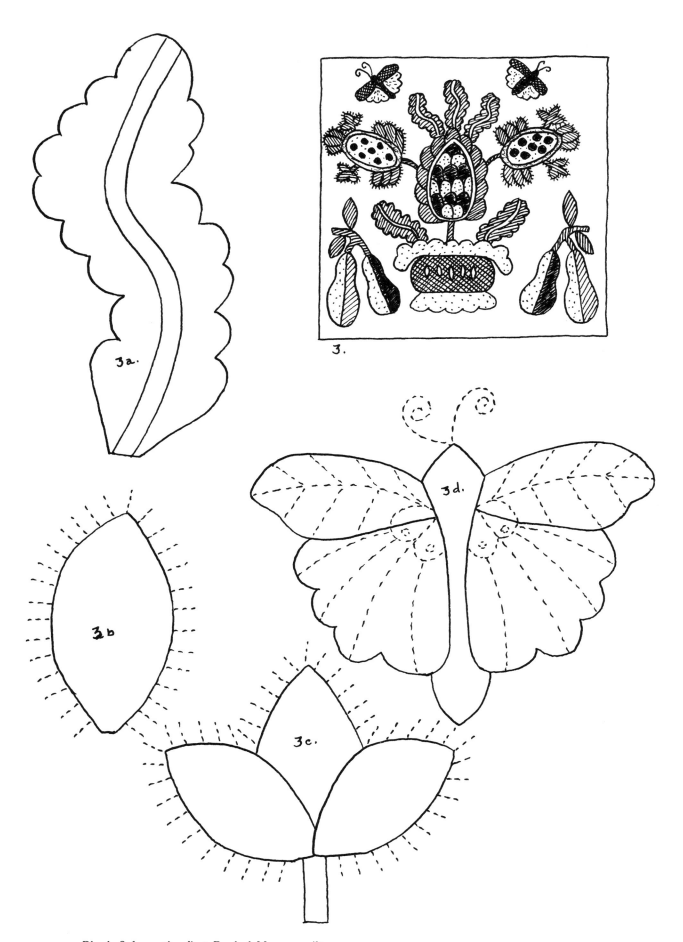

Block 3 from the first Rachel Meyer quilt.

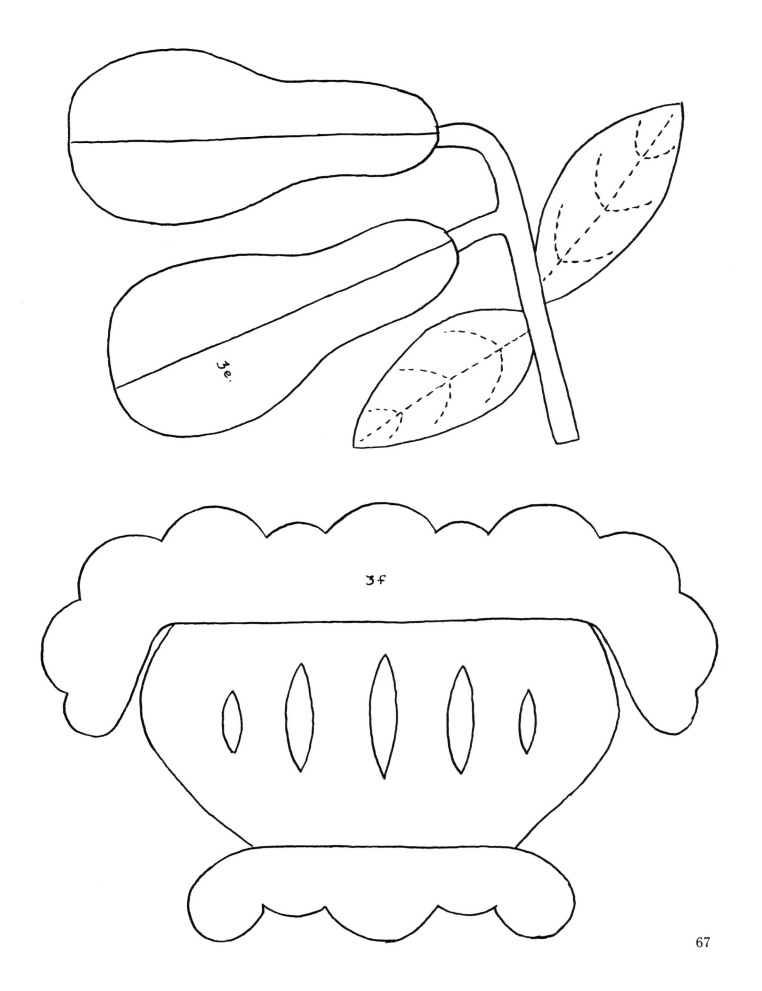

3e.

3f

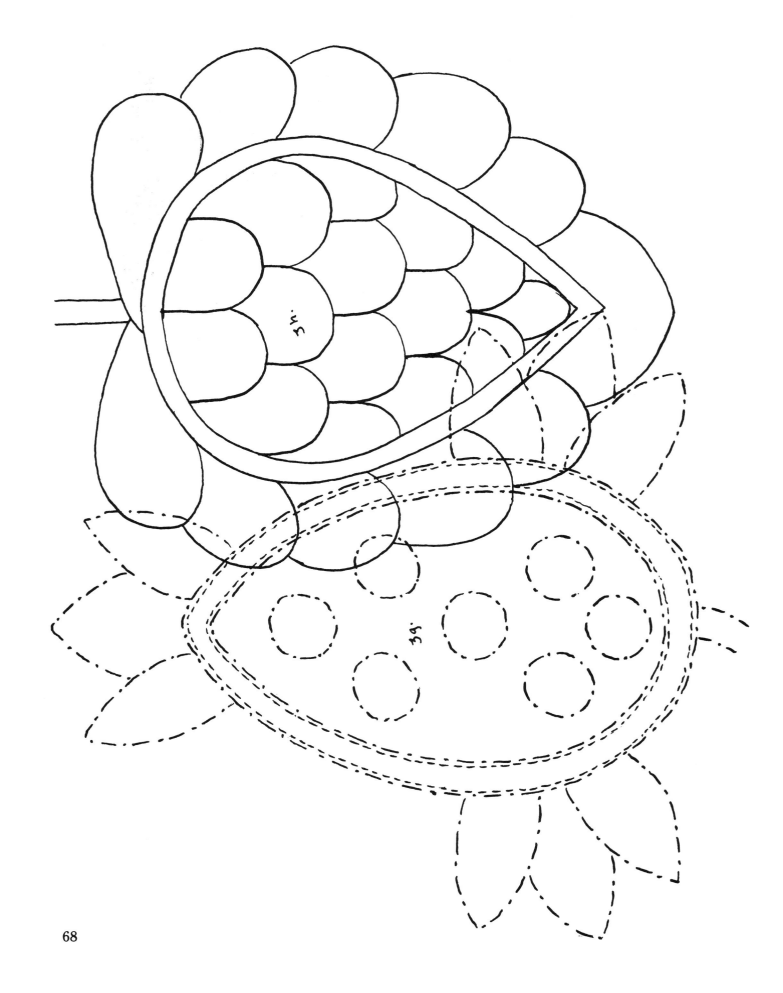

68

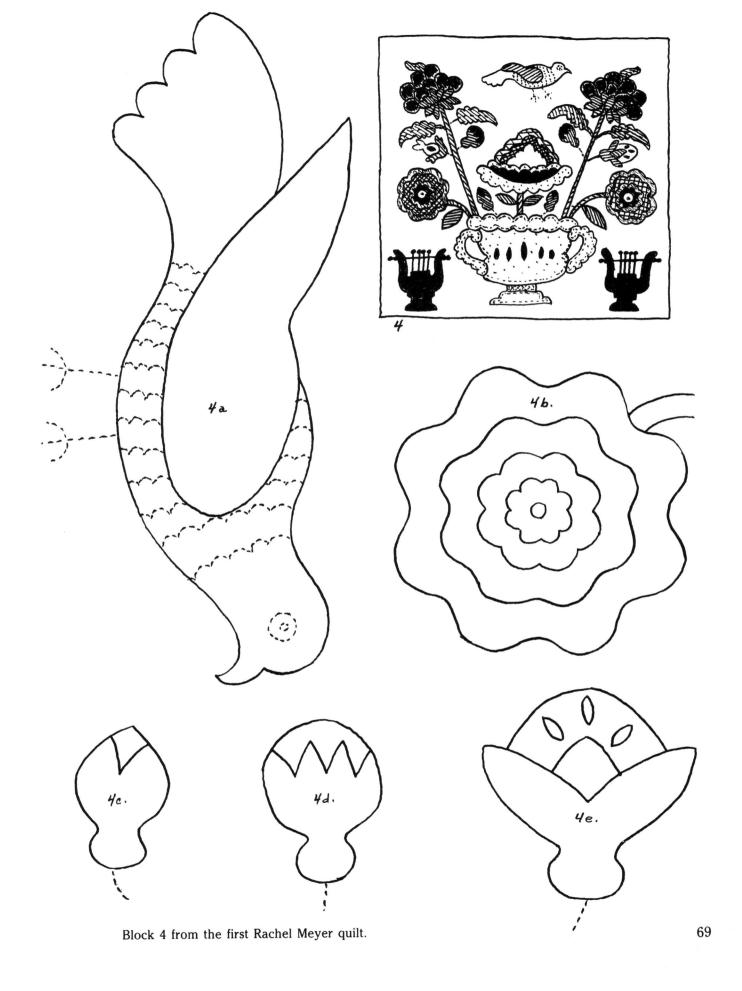

4a

4b.

4

4c.

4d.

4e.

Block 4 from the first Rachel Meyer quilt.

4g.

4h.

4j.

4k

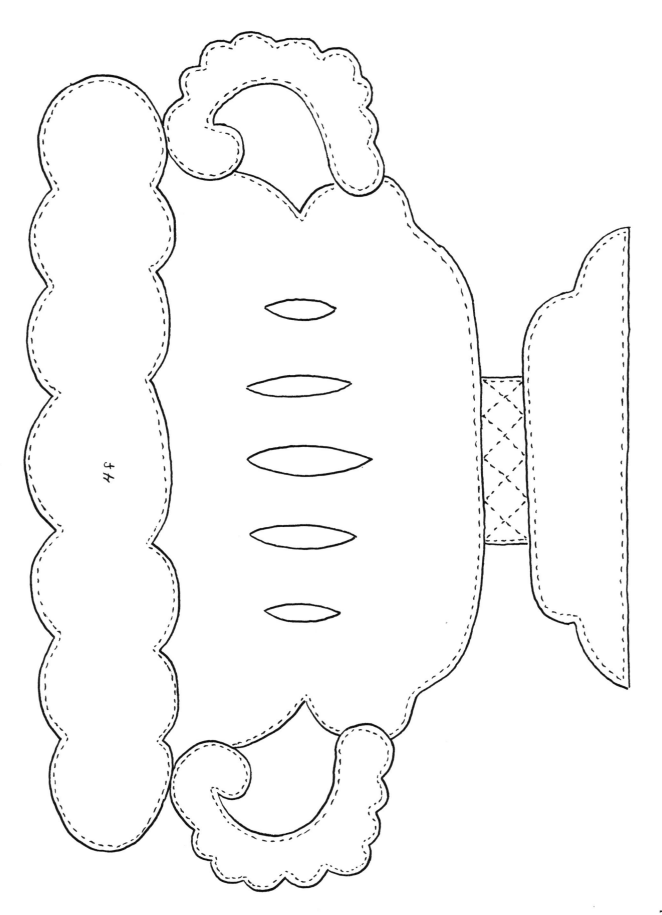

71

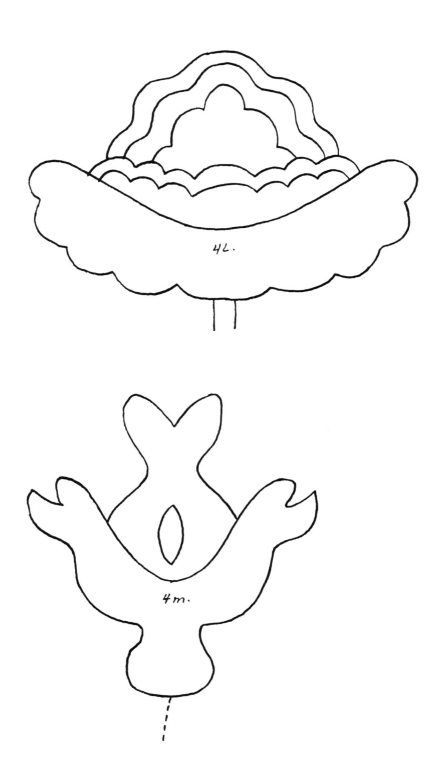

4L.

4m.

72

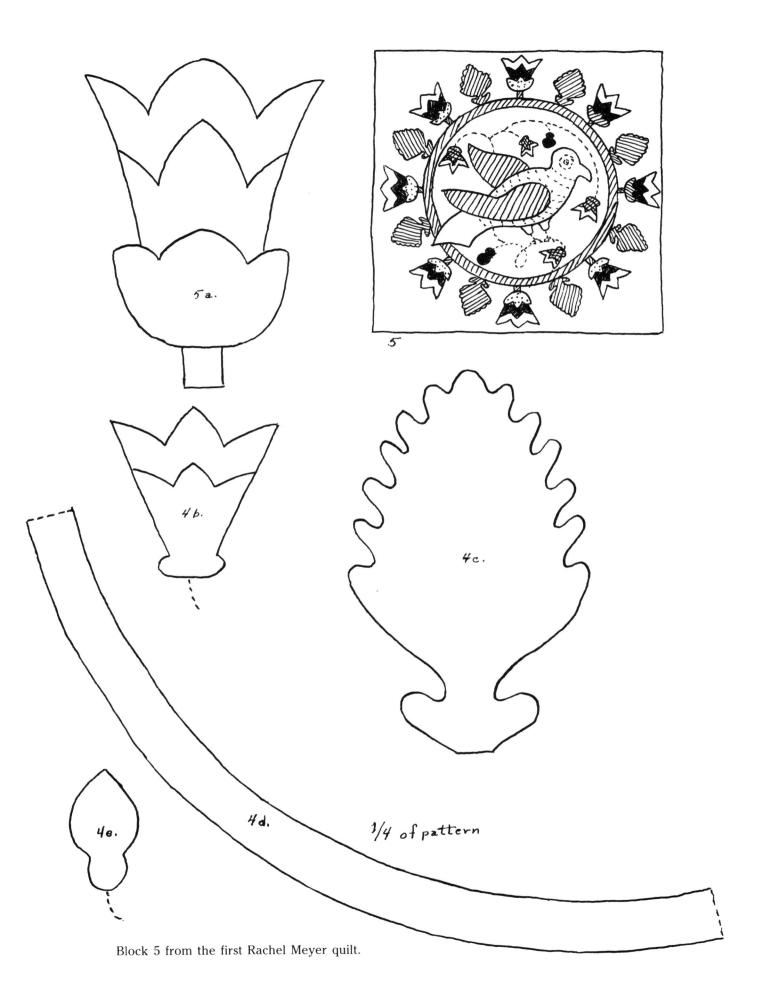

5a.

5

4b.

4c.

4e.

4d.

1/4 of pattern

Block 5 from the first Rachel Meyer quilt.

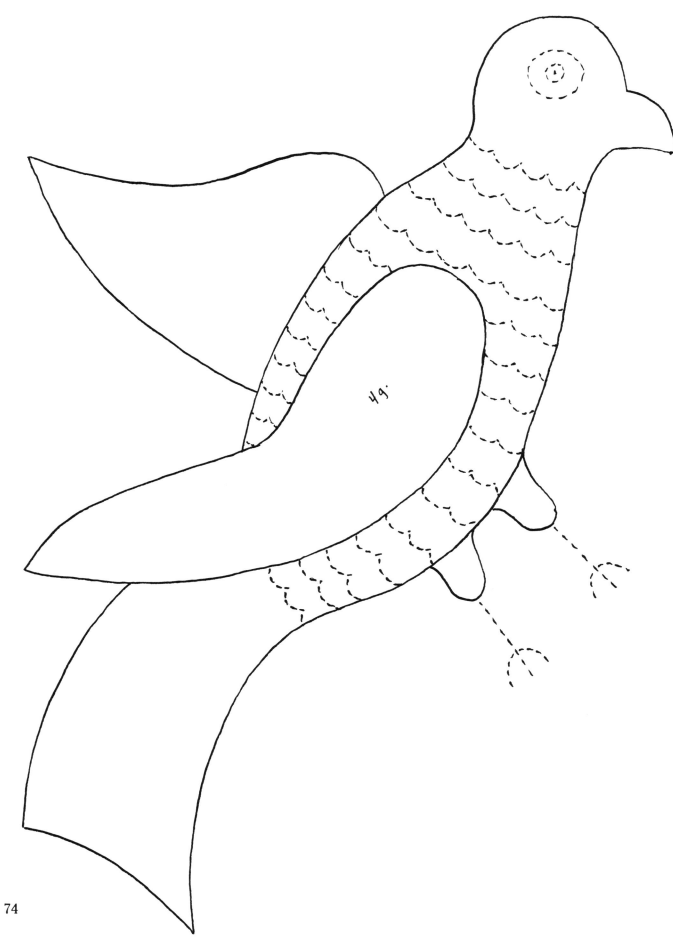

49.

6a.

6b.

6c.

6d.

6e

6

75

Block 6 from the first Rachel Meyer quilt.

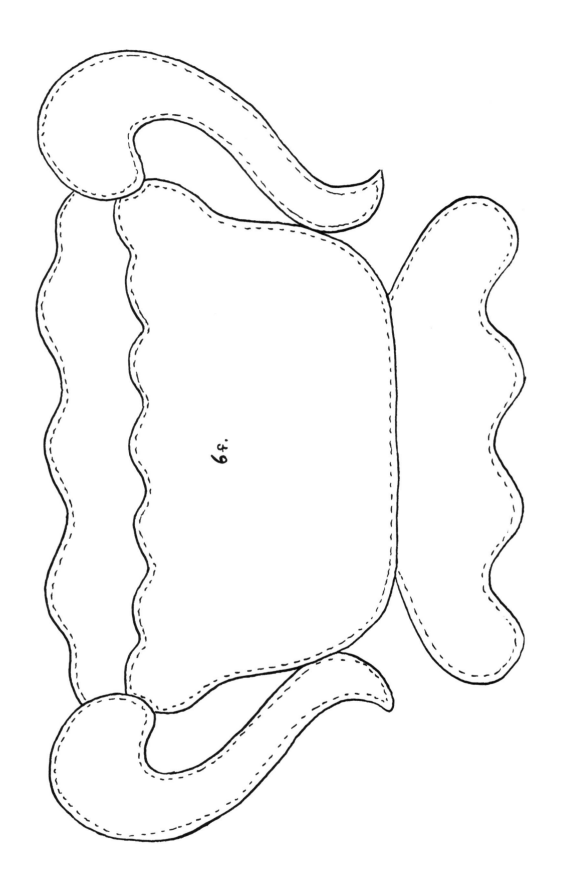

69.

76

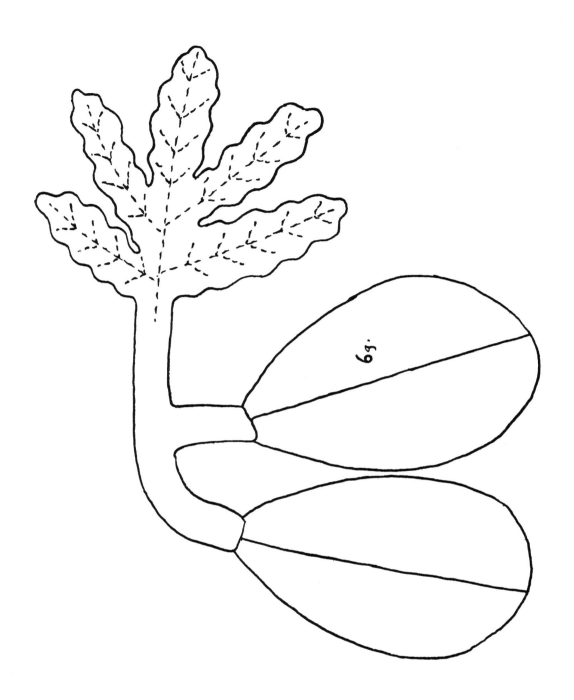

69.

77

6h.

6j.

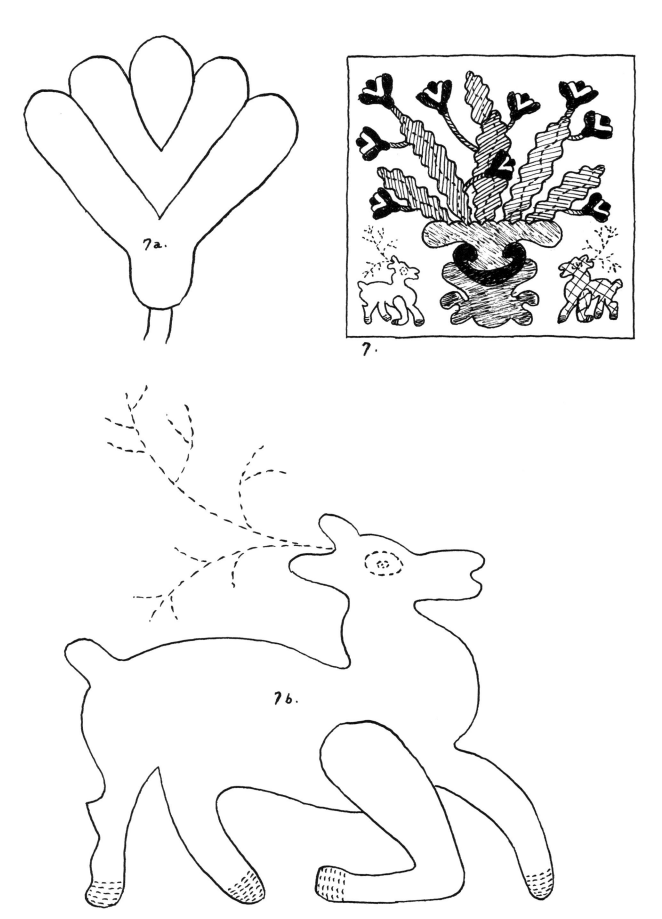

Block 7 from the first Rachel Meyer quilt.

7c.

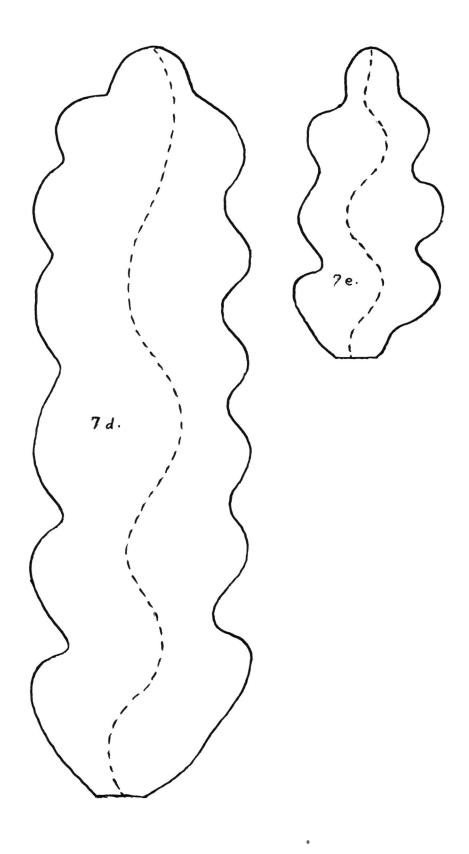

7 d.

7 e.

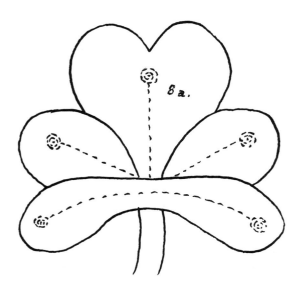

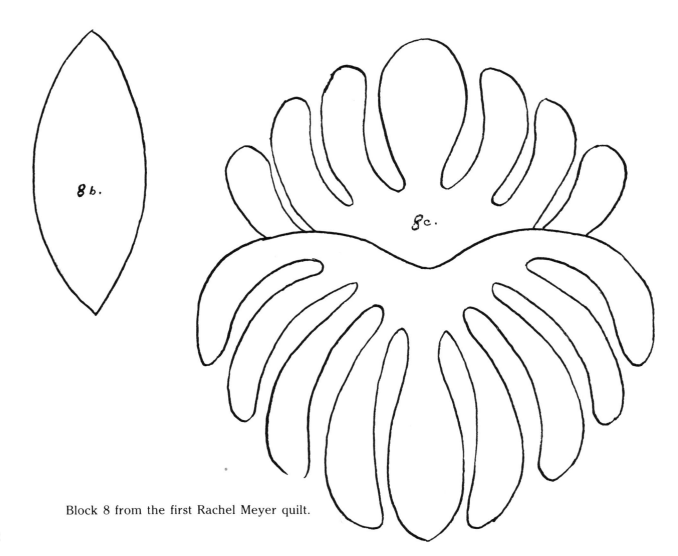

Block 8 from the first Rachel Meyer quilt.

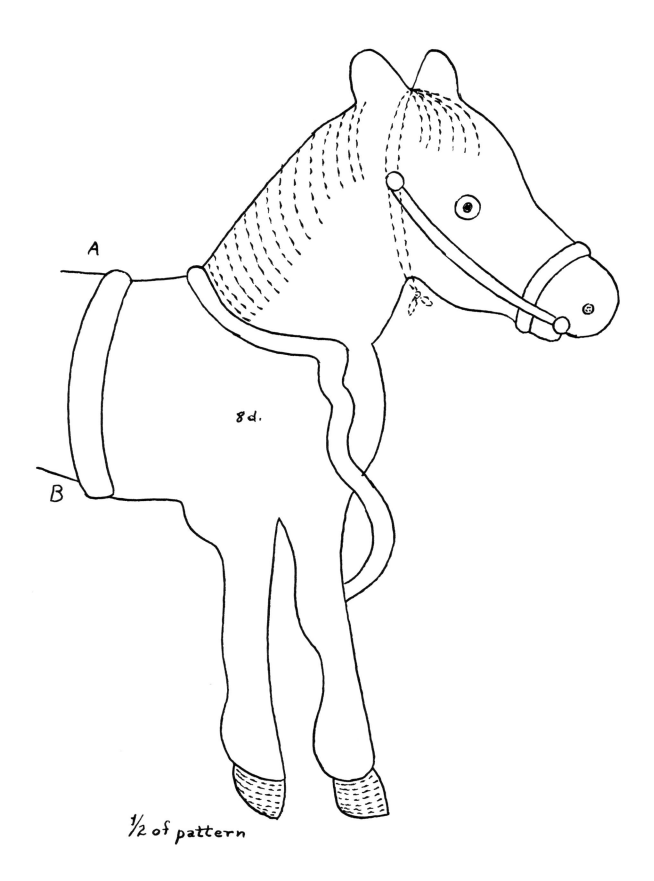

A

B

8 d.

½ of pattern

A

8 d.

B

½ of pattern

8e.

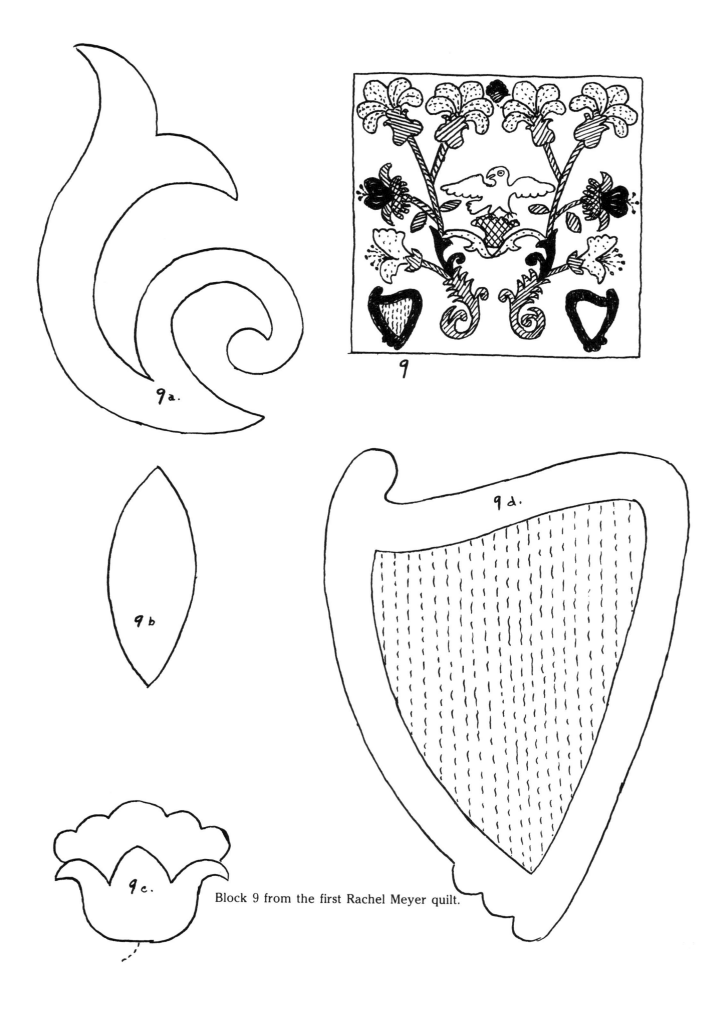

9a.

9

9 b

9 c.

9 d.

Block 9 from the first Rachel Meyer quilt.

9 f

9 e

9 g.

86

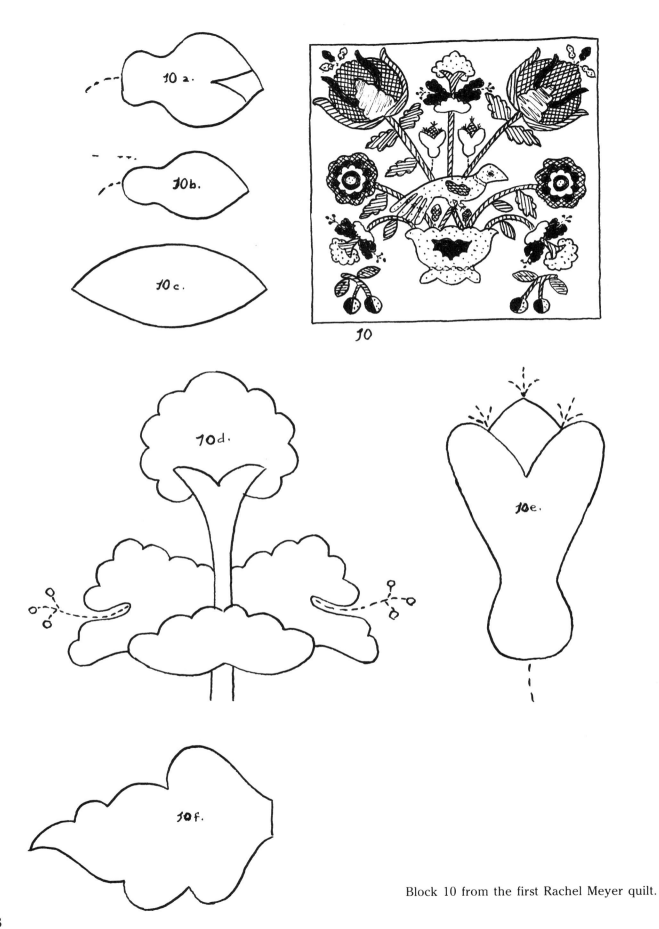

10 a.

10b.

10 c.

10

10d.

10e.

10 f.

Block 10 from the first Rachel Meyer quilt.

88

10 h.

30.

89

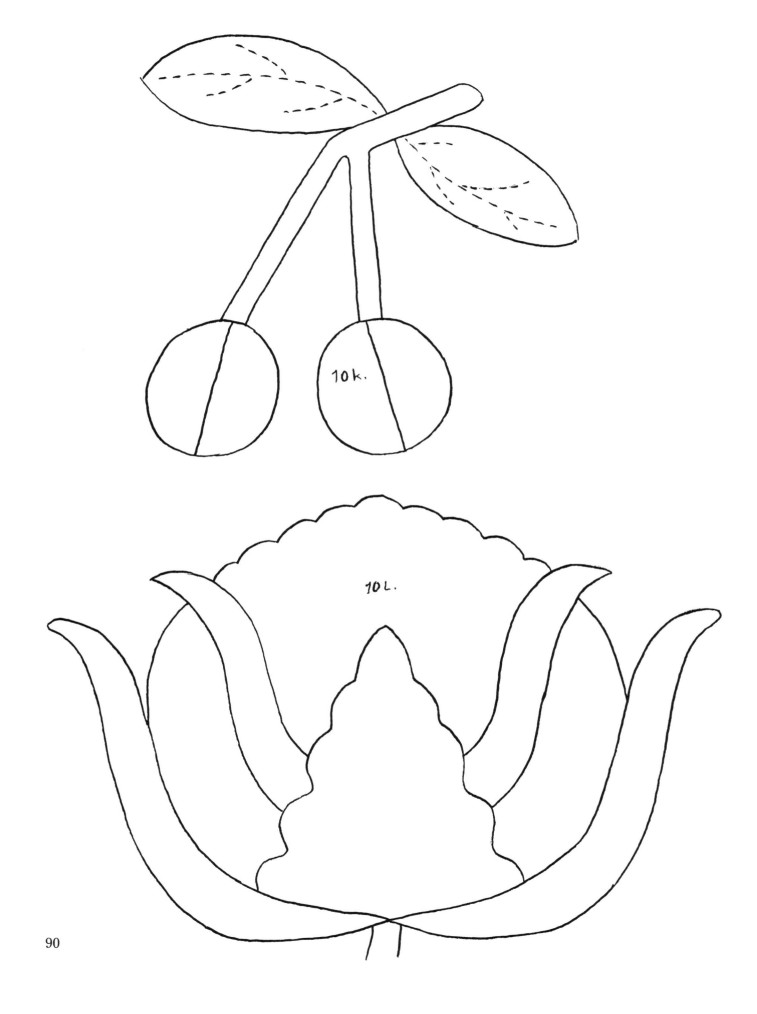

10k.

10L.

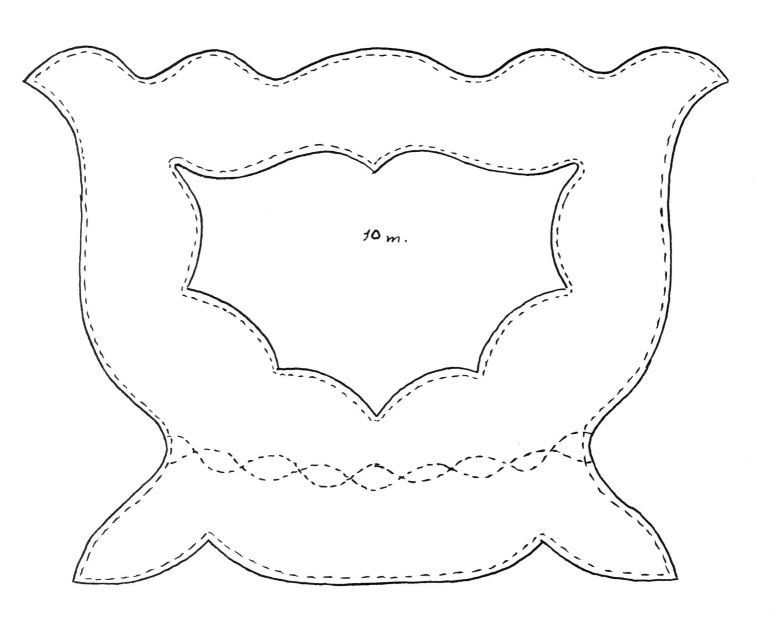

10 m.

11

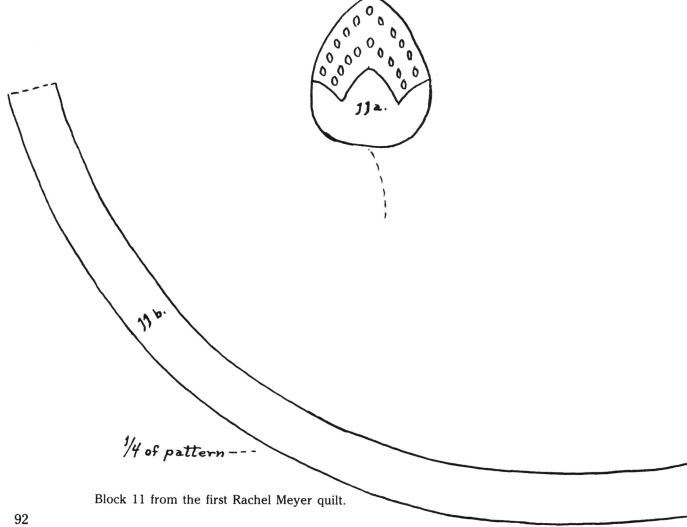

11 a.

11 b.

¼ of pattern - - -

Block 11 from the first Rachel Meyer quilt.

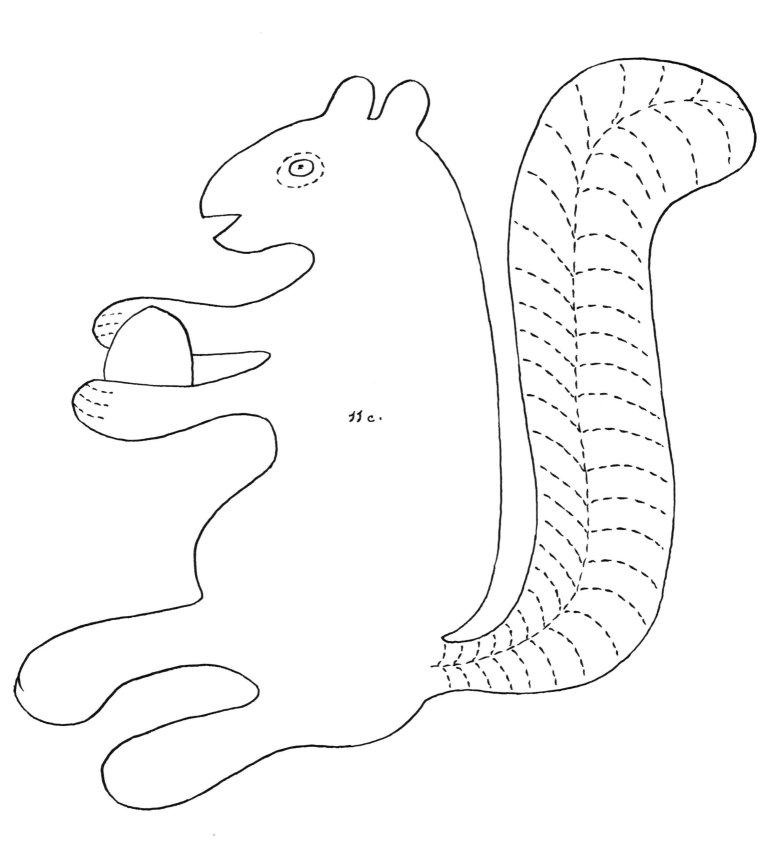

11c.

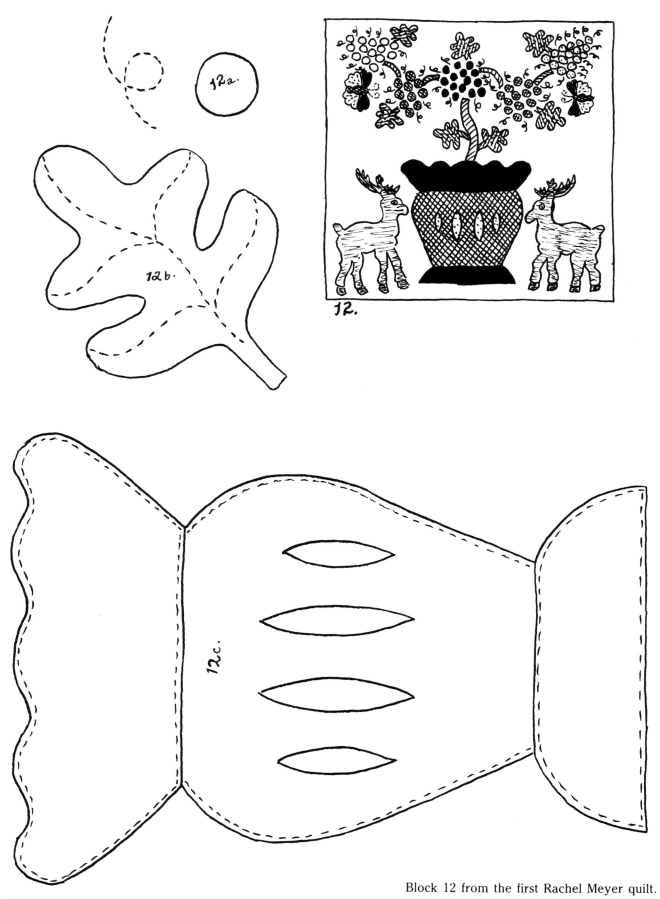

Block 12 from the first Rachel Meyer quilt.

12 d.

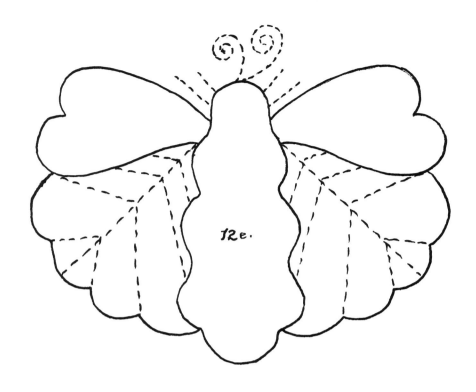

12e.

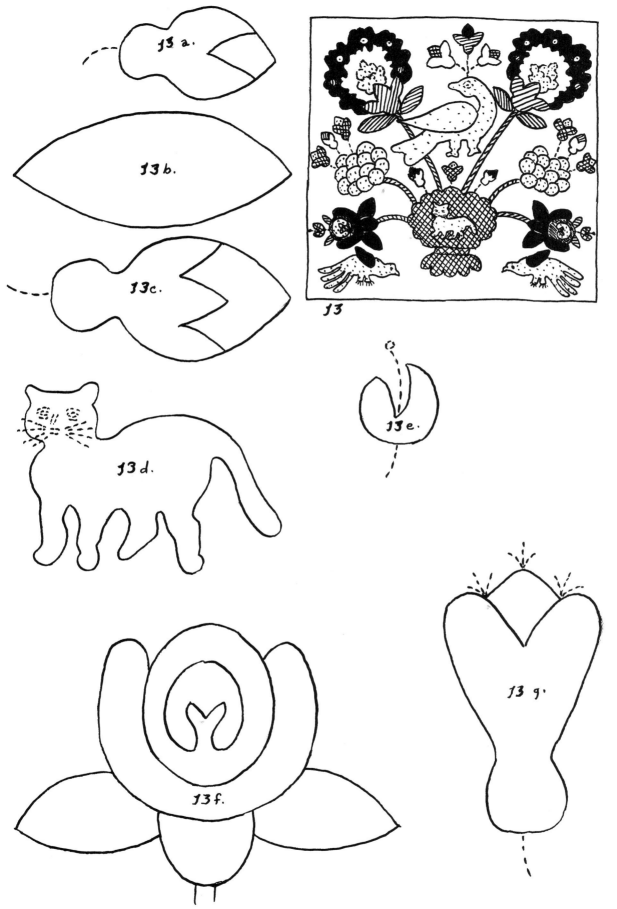

13 a.

13 b.

13 c.

13

13 d.

13 e.

13 f.

13 g.

Block 13 from the first Rachel Meyer quilt.

13h.

13 s.

13 k.

13 L.

Border section and flowers from the first Rachel Meyer quilt.

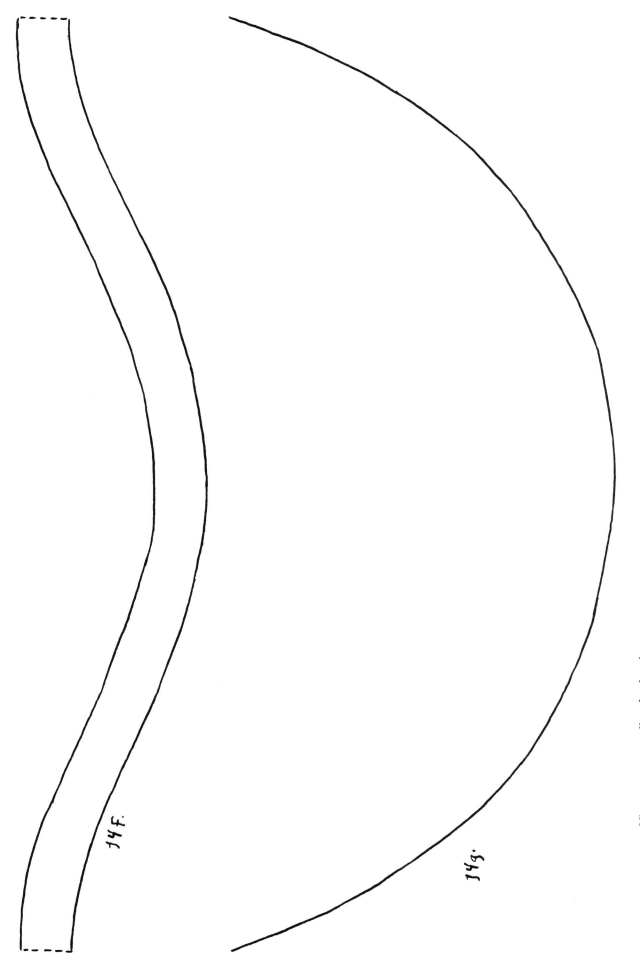

14 f.

14 g.

Vine pattern; scallop for border.

3

An Early Victorian Quilt

As the quilt in Chapter 2 was a perfect expression of the Chinese export period of the Federal Era, so this quilt is a perfect expression of the early Victorian period in the United States.

Mrs. Rachel Meyer made this quilt (Picture 6) as well as the quilt in Chapter 2 (Picture 5), and her work again shows careful planning of the motifs and lovely stitches. Many things in this quilt, which was made at least ten years after the first quilt, indicate that Mrs. Meyer had changed. She put as much work into creating beauty as before, but her viewpoint had changed and matured. Fewer motifs are worked into the top and those used are combined in more unified designs. The quilting has motifs that are as important to the finished quilt as the appliqué. In discussing the first quilt, I barely mentioned the quilting, which was outline quilting and merely held the three layers of the quilt together without adding to its beauty.

This later quilt is red and green on white. The white is still homespun, similar to the background cloth in the first quilt. The green is also the yellowish-green home-dyed cloth similar to that in the first quilt, but the red is different. The red cloth of the first quilt began to wear very quickly and it must have taught Mrs. Meyer to pay more for her cloth to ensure better quality, for this cloth has kept its bright color and has worn very little.

We cannot assume that the circumstances of the Meyer family had improved simply because Mrs. Meyer paid more for the cloth she used in this quilt, since we cannot know how long it may have taken her to save the money for this expense. It is the combination of better red cloth and the use of one of the very new sewing machines that tells us that the fami-

ly was now able to afford some luxuries. The appliqué and quilting were still done by hand, as they had been in the first quilt, but Mrs. Meyer used a sewing machine to imitate the fine chain stitch embroidery so profuse on her earlier quilt. Perhaps failing eyesight necessitated this imitation. The fineness of her former work would be difficult to execute without almost perfect sight.

The first sewing machines effected a chain stitch until the shuttle was invented, allowing the two-thread lock stitch which has been used ever since. This two-thread machine was invented in 1846 and was put on the market soon afterwards. Its popularity overtook that of the chain stitch machine as soon as its obvious advantages became evident. We cannot date the quilt from this, however, since Mrs. Meyer may have purchased the machine at any time before this innovation became available or she may have purchased a secondhand machine at any time afterwards. She was only interested in the chain stitch for use as outline embroidery.

Mrs. Meyer again made an outstanding border for her quilt. Although similar to the borders popular in the 1840s and 1850s, the perfect proportion, in both size and color, of the border to the designs in the body of the quilt makes it difficult to visualize the quilt without this exact border.

Mrs. Meyer's quilts are both such perfect early American graphic quilts and perfect individual expressions of an artistic personality that the study of all American graphic quilts is enriched by their inclusion. The second quilt belongs to Mrs. Louis K. Beckley, a cousin of Mrs. Henry Hecht who owns the first quilt. These ladies are both direct descendants of Mrs. Meyer and live in Baltimore.

Picture 6 Second Rachel Meyer quilt in the 1840-1845 Victorian, Baltimore style. By permission of Mrs. Louis K. Beckley, owner.

Motifs

The motif in the middle block of the top row has a red hunting horn with flowers and sprays of buds sprouting from it (*See* Figure 137). The horn has a green chain stitch outline and a green, gray, and red twisted cord tied in a bow with green appliquéd tassel ends. This cord is also made of chain stitch but has three threads used together. There are two satin stitch stars embroidered on thin cloth which were cut out and then appliquéd in place. These are green with red outlines. On the top is a peony-like flower in red with a gray outline and green base. The next two flowers are white with melon outlines and green leaves. The buds are green with green outlines and the final buds are red on green leaves.

With her remarkable attention to detail, Mrs. Meyer has given the quilt a unity of design along with variety. The basis of the motifs is flowers in bouquets and sprays, yet there are single flowers and birds worked into the motifs for emphasis. The colors are basically red and green on white, the most popular color combination of the 1840s. It was used in hundreds of quilts, yet Mrs. Meyer was enough of an artist to take this basic color combination and work in slight touches of brown, blue, melon, and peach, enlivening the basic colors without drawing attention from them.

In the top row, the center block does not have the same yellow-green leaves and elements as all the other blocks. The leaves and green elements in this block are blue-green. Adding this one patch with dark leaves illustrates the superstition common among quilters at that time, namely that "Only God can make a perfect thing and a human who presumed to create something perfect would call down the wrath of Heaven." This superstition was Chinese and was brought into this country with the Chinese export wares. In this country, it became a means for quilters to brag that in making their quilts, women had to consciously avoid perfection.

One of the most interesting aspects of this quilt is the tiny embroidered designs which are appliquéd to the vases. It is dumbfounding to see these designs on an 1840s quilt because they are so much like the machine-embroidery motifs you can buy today at the notions counter of any department store. However, they are completely handmade in the smallest stitches imaginable. Mrs. Meyer made them in satin and seed stitch and a few tiny French knots on a foundation of very fine netting. She then cut them out and appliquéd them to the quilt blocks. I have drawn the motifs in Figure 138 to their exact size. The stars (5a and 5b) were used on the hunting horn as already stated. The flower and bud (1a and 1b) are from the first block in the second row. The flower is dark red with a peach-colored center and the buds are dark red, while all of the leaves are green. The flower (2) is from the lower right-hand block of the quilt. This flower has pale blue petals and a brown and peach center with green stems and leaves. The next flower and bud set (3a and 3b) is from the second block of the third row. The flower has pinkish rose petals with a brown and peach center, while the buds have two brown sections. Again, all of the leaves are green. The flower and bud, labeled 4a and 4b, come from the left-hand block of the last row. This is definitely a rose and a rose leaf. The flower is a pale blue satin stitch around a cluster of the very finest French knots in brown. There are four tiny blue stitches at the tip of the bud and all of the leaves are green.

The last motifs to be considered in this quilt are the quilting motifs and their relation to the rest of the patterns used. Three motifs are used in the quilting, but two of them are modifications of each other. In the squares formed by the meeting of the white lattice strips, there is a dainty medallion with a round center and four tulips that project a few inches into the lattice strips, forming a pretty corner for the appliqué squares.

Forming a frame for the appliqué blocks are strips of straight feather quilting placed on the lattice strips between the tulip medallions. Four of these strips are placed the length of the opening in the center of the corner swags of the border.

Mrs. Meyer finished the sides of her quilt top with half-tulip medallions in the corners. Between these are half-feathers showing that the lattice strips at the edges of the center top are one and one-half inches wide rather than three inches, as the others are. Mrs. Meyer must have started her quilting in the corner of the upper right-hand side because the quarter medallion and two half-feathers are missing from the quilting in this corner and the half-feathers are missing from the top edge of the center.

The space between the top of the appliquéd border and the edge of the quilt center is filled in with curved feathers that are 16 inches long and curve to fill a space six and three-quarter inches wide. The outer edge of the quilt is finished with a straight feather. The background quilting is diagonal lines. In part of

Figure 137 Block 2, center of upper row in the second Rachel Meyer quilt.

the quilt, these lines go from right to left and in the remainder they go from left to right.

As Mrs. Meyer quilted the top, she also stuffed extra cotton in all of the appliquéd motifs except the leaves and the swag. This is called padding and allows the motifs to stand out in high relief from the rest of the quilting.

In this second quilt, the quilting is of much more importance to the finished design of the top. The stitches are as tiny in this quilt as in the first, but neither is the hand as steady nor the eye as sure. These two examples of Mrs. Meyer's quilts leave me with a longing to see more of her work and the wish that more of her quilts had lasted the approximately 150 years since she made them.

The finished size patterns for Mrs. Meyer's second quilt are on the following pages. The twelve blocks are 18 inches square plus a one-quarter-inch seam

Picture 6 Second Rachel Meyer quilt.

allowance on all four sides. The border may be cut in 18-inch-wide strips or it may also be done in 18-inch-square blocks. The dotted lines marked with letters and arrows show how to join the sections of the larger patterns. The dotted lines outlining the motifs show where the embroidery is placed on the blocks. For several of the blocks, no patterns for stems are given. This allows for individual placement of the different elements. You may make the stems using either thin appliqués or lines of embroidery.

To make the side swags, use the two patterns marked 13e and their reverse; join them where indicated by the dotted lines. To make the corner swags, use the larger pattern 13e and its reverse (sides) and pattern 13f and its reverse (center), joined as indicated along the dotted lines. To sew the corner and side swags, cut all the pieces out first. Pin the green center pieces in place, with the ends touching, all the way around the border. Be sure to leave enough room at the top and bottom of the border strip for the other pieces of the swags. Baste the center pieces in place when you are sure they are all positioned correctly. The seam allowances should not be folded under on these pieces. One at a time, lay the red strips that belong above the centers in place along the pencil lines of the green centers. Fold the seam allowance of the red strip under on the side touching the green center. Appliqué this strip along the side that touches the green center; baste the other side in place with the seam allowance unfolded. Repeat for the red strip below the green center, all the way around the border. The green outer strips are sewn in the same way, only for these strips both seam allowances are folded under and appliquéd in place.

Figure 138 Embroidery motifs from the second Rachel Meyer quilt.

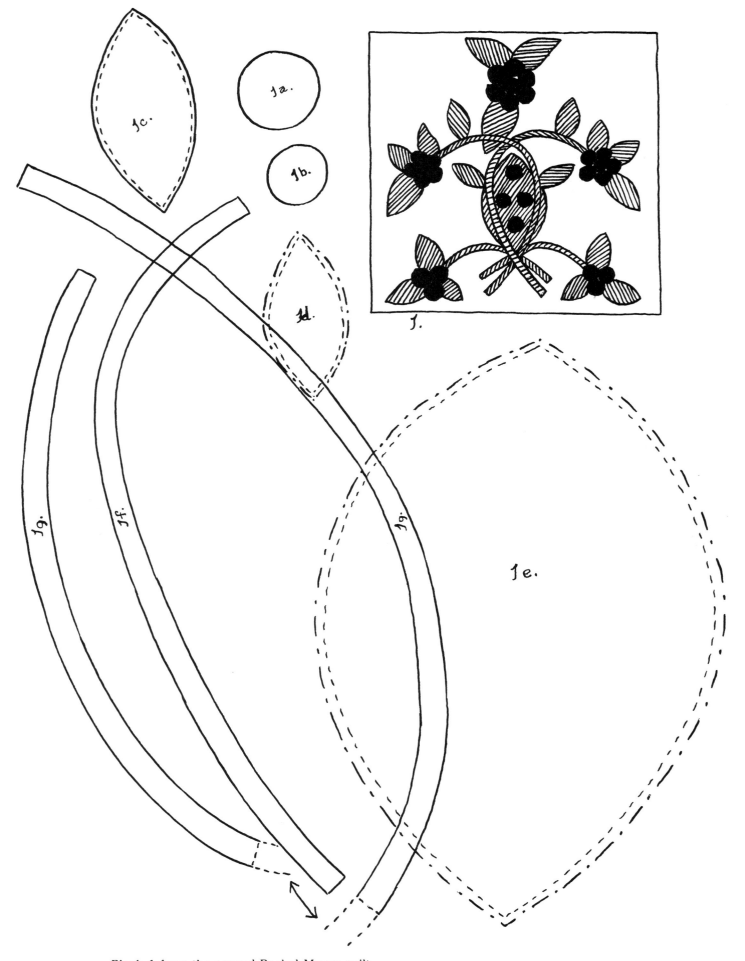

Block 1 from the second Rachel Meyer quilt.

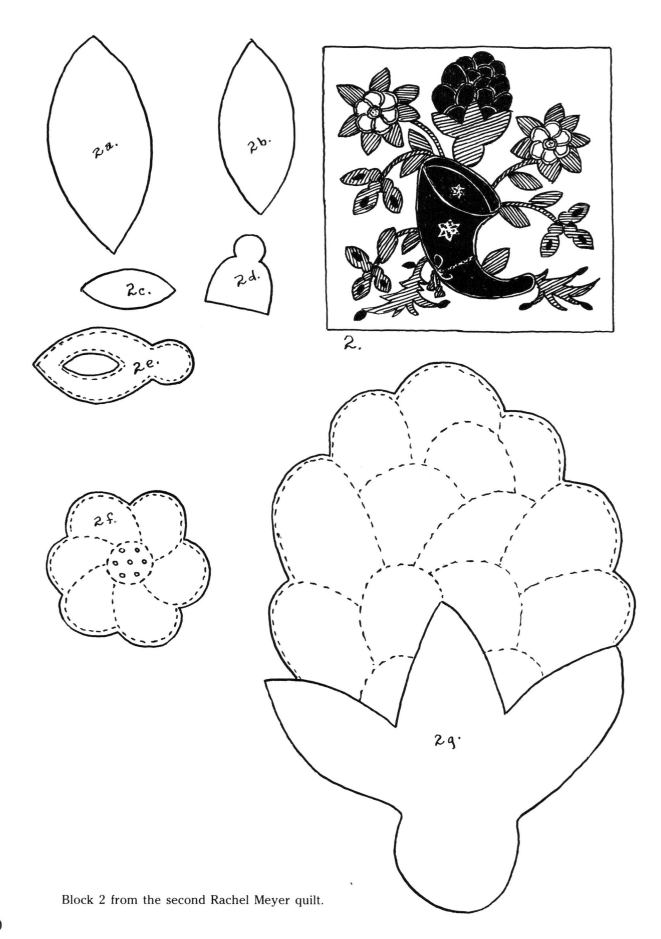

2a.

2b.

2c.

2d.

2e.

2.

2f.

2g.

Block 2 from the second Rachel Meyer quilt.

110

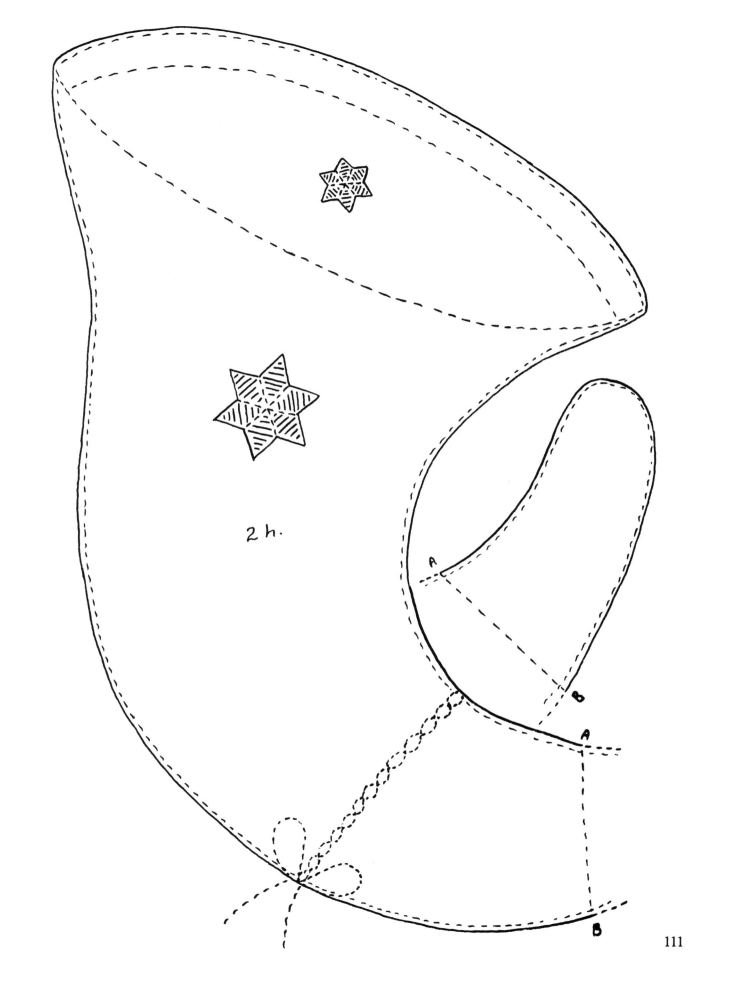

2 h.

A

B

A

B

111

2j

2k

2l.

112

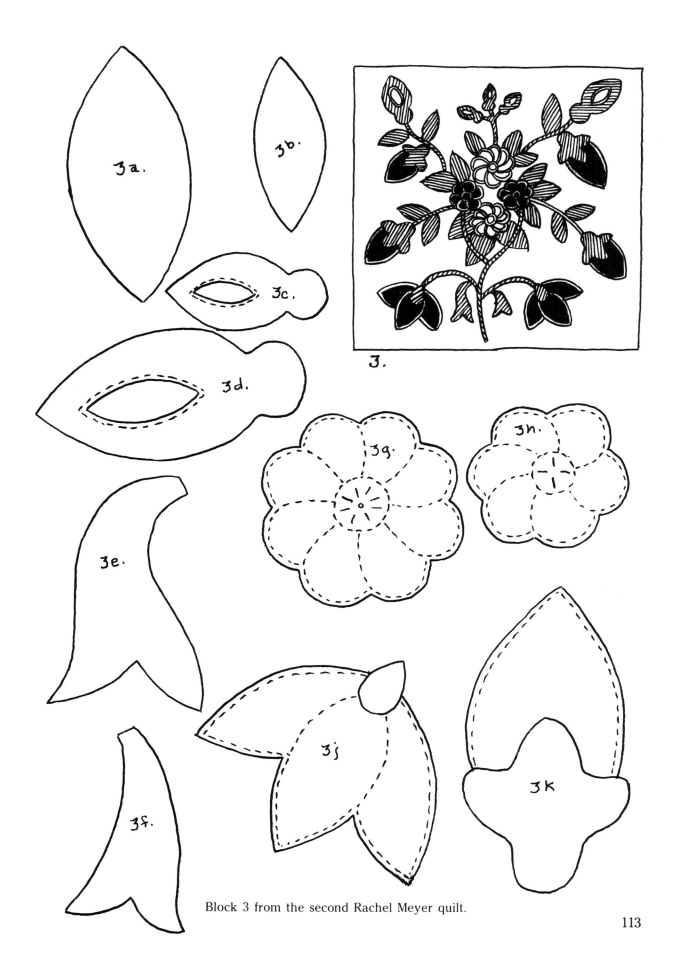

3a.

3b.

3c.

3d.

3.

3e.

3g.

3h.

3f.

3j.

3k

Block 3 from the second Rachel Meyer quilt.

113

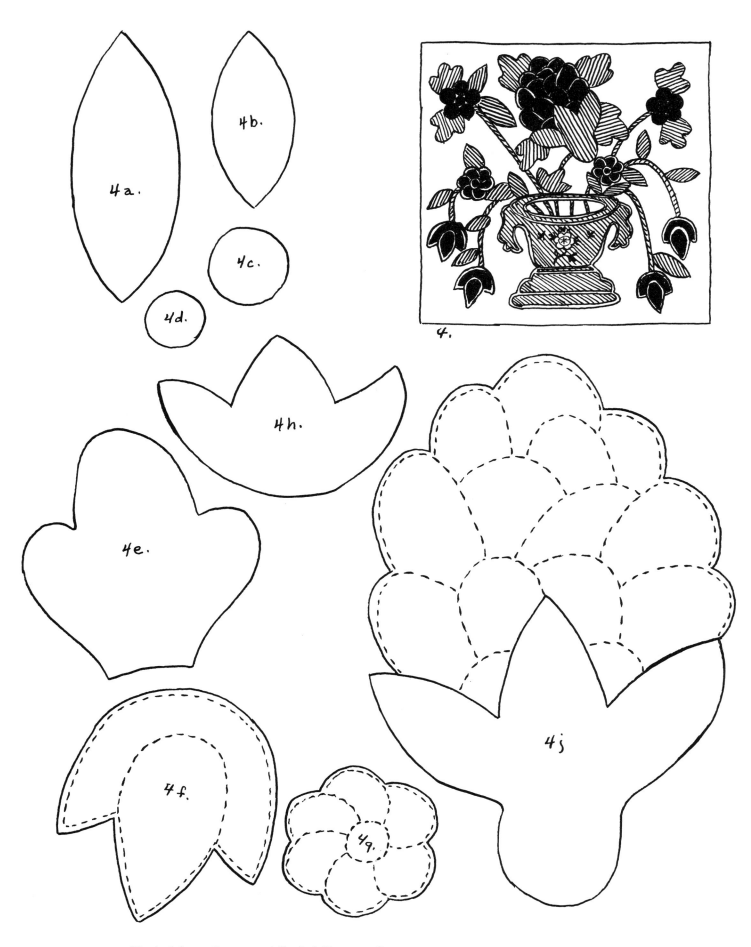

4a.

4b.

4c.

4d.

4.

4h.

4e.

4j.

4f.

4g.

Block 4 from the second Rachel Meyer quilt.

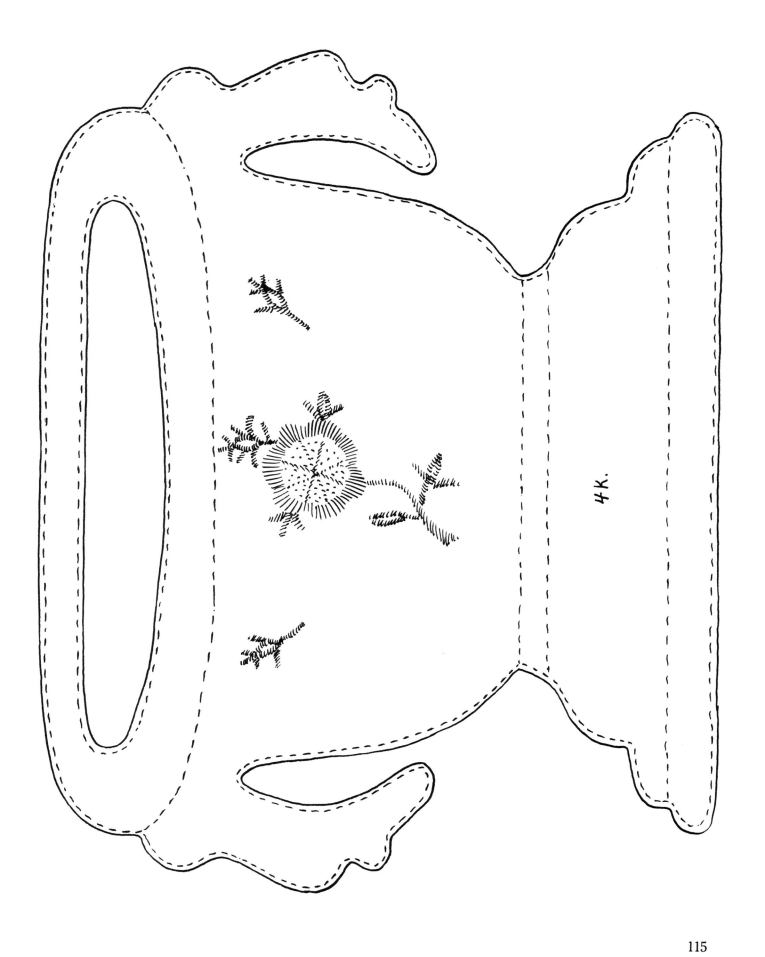

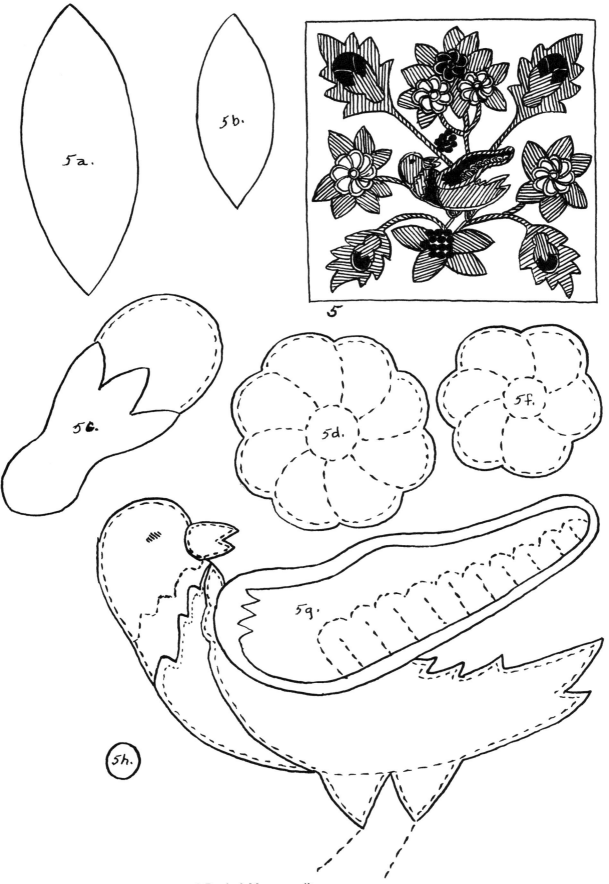

Block 5 from the second Rachel Meyer quilt.

116

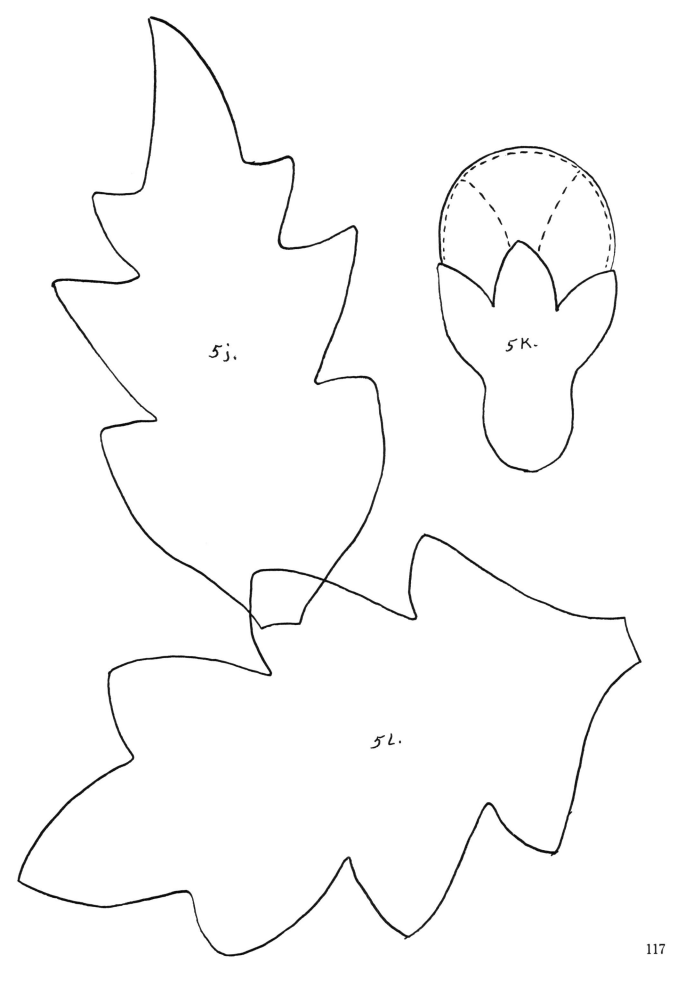

5 j.

5 K.

5 L.

117

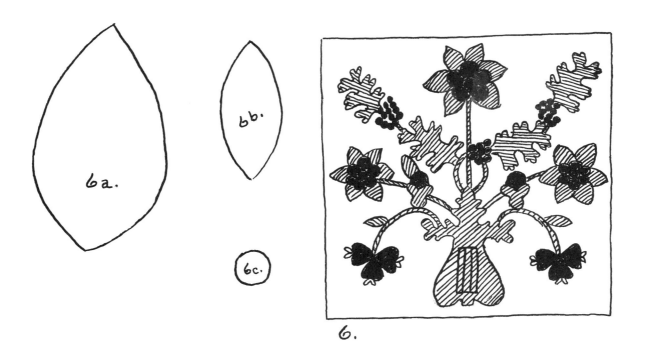

6a.

6b.

6c.

6.

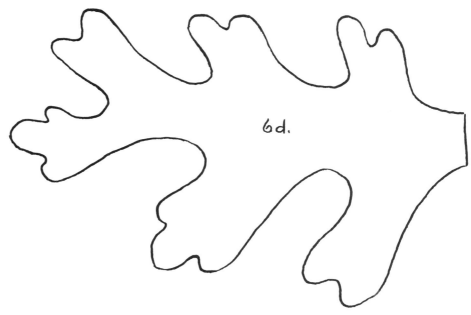

6d.

Block 6 from the second Rachel Meyer quilt.

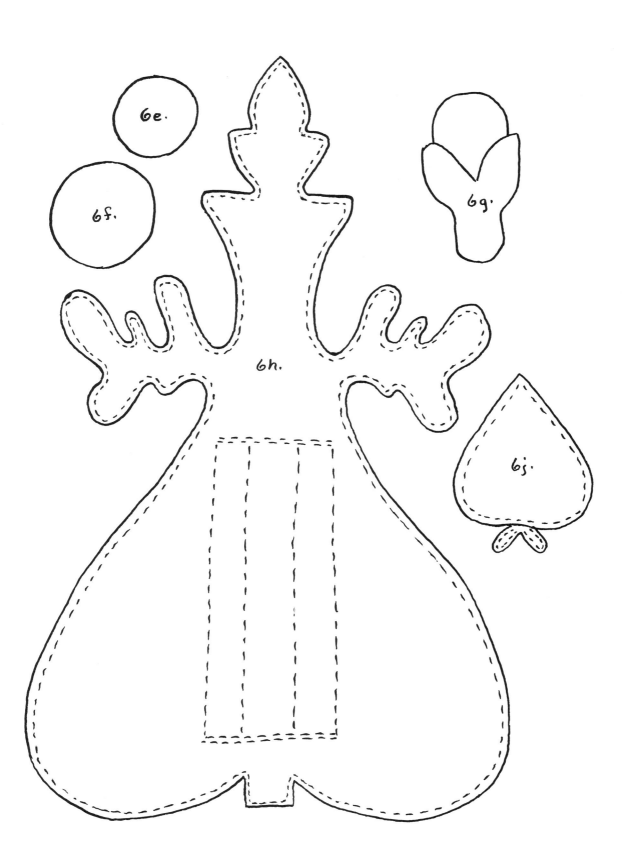

6e.

6f.

6g.

6h.

6j.

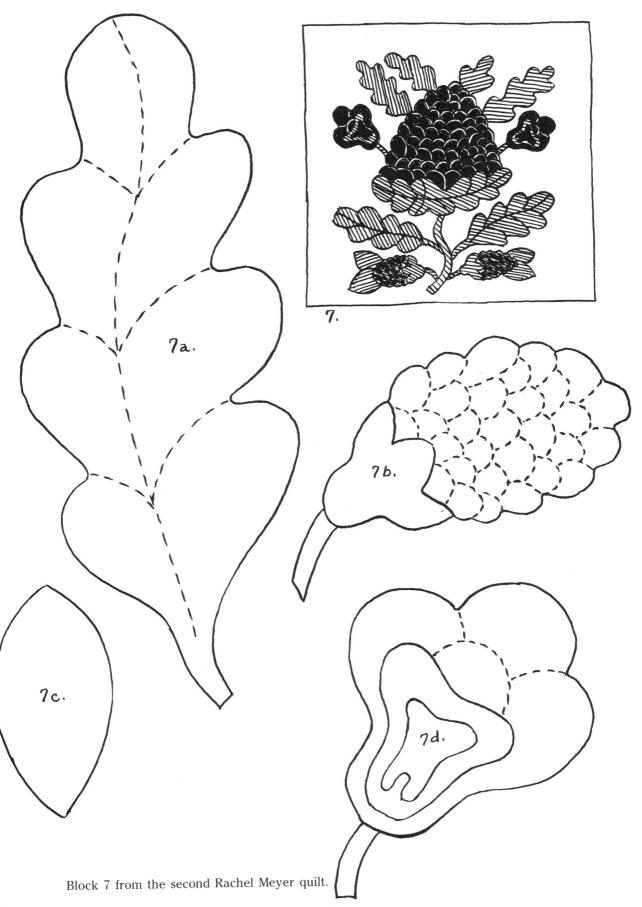

7a.

7.

7b.

7c.

7d.

Block 7 from the second Rachel Meyer quilt.

7e.

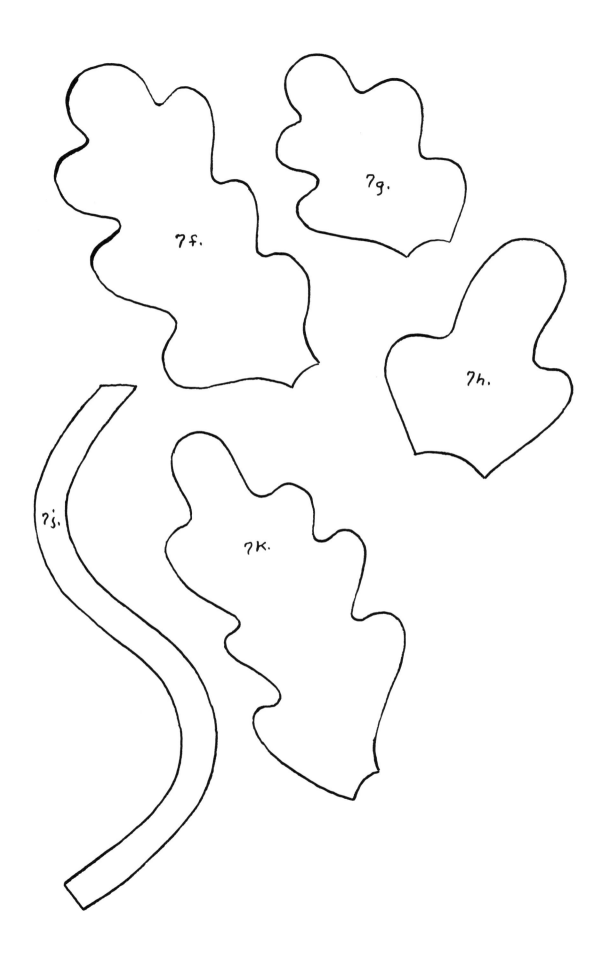

7f.

7g.

7h.

7j.

7k.

122

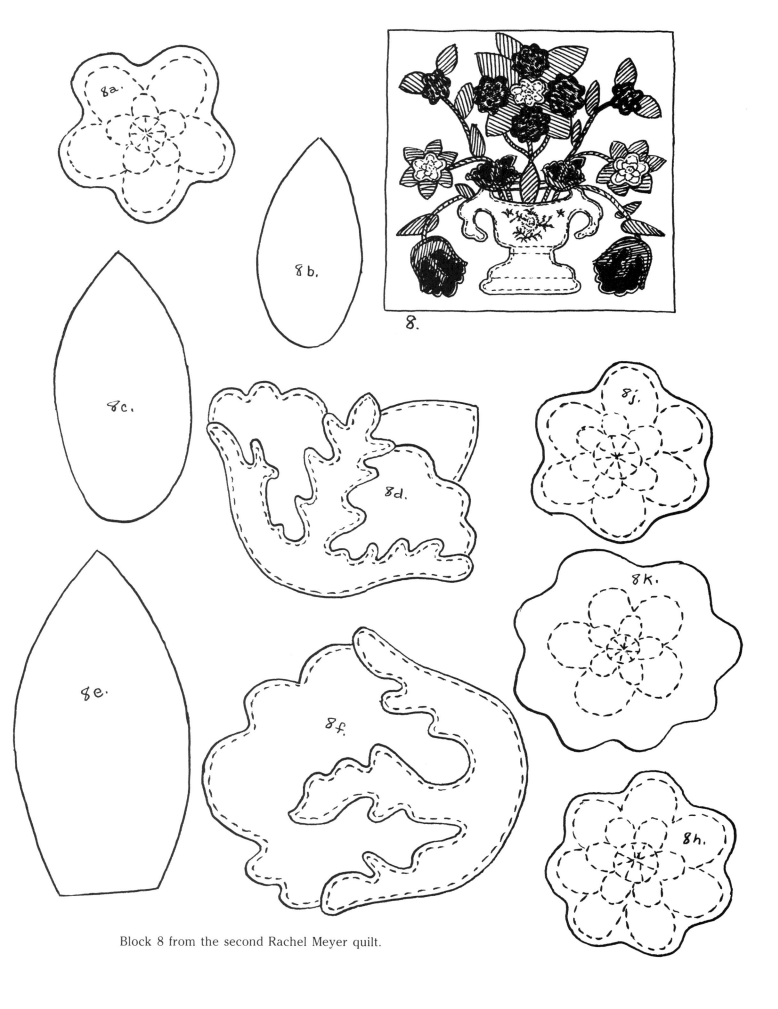

8a.

8b.

8.

8c.

8d.

8j.

8k.

8e.

8f.

8h.

Block 8 from the second Rachel Meyer quilt.

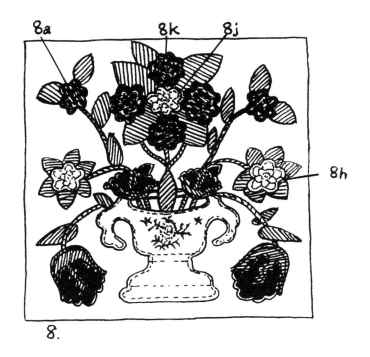

8a 8k 8j

8h

8.

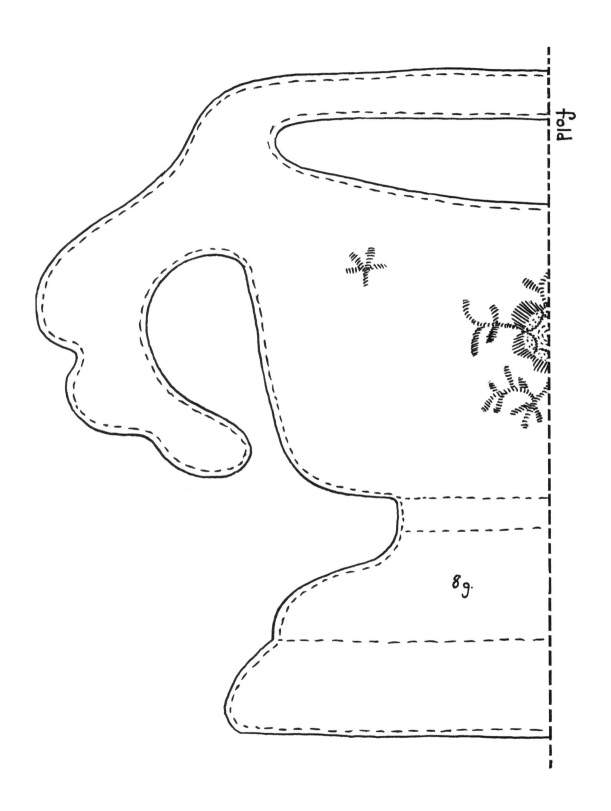

Fold

89.

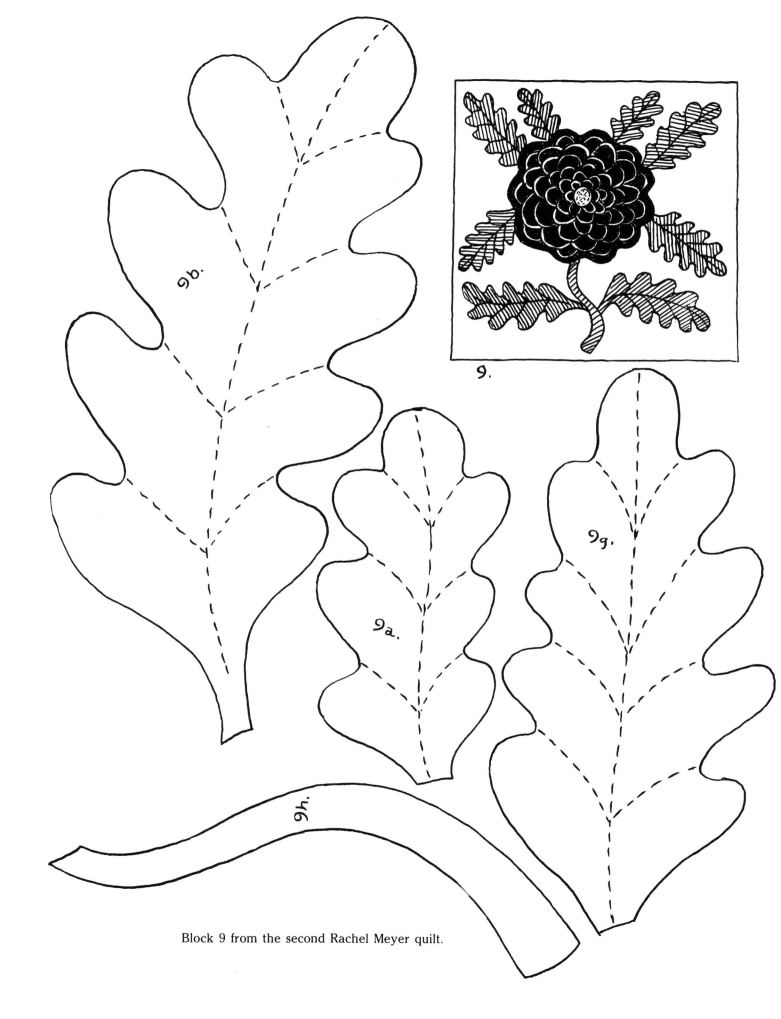

9b.

9.

9g.

9a.

9h.

Block 9 from the second Rachel Meyer quilt.

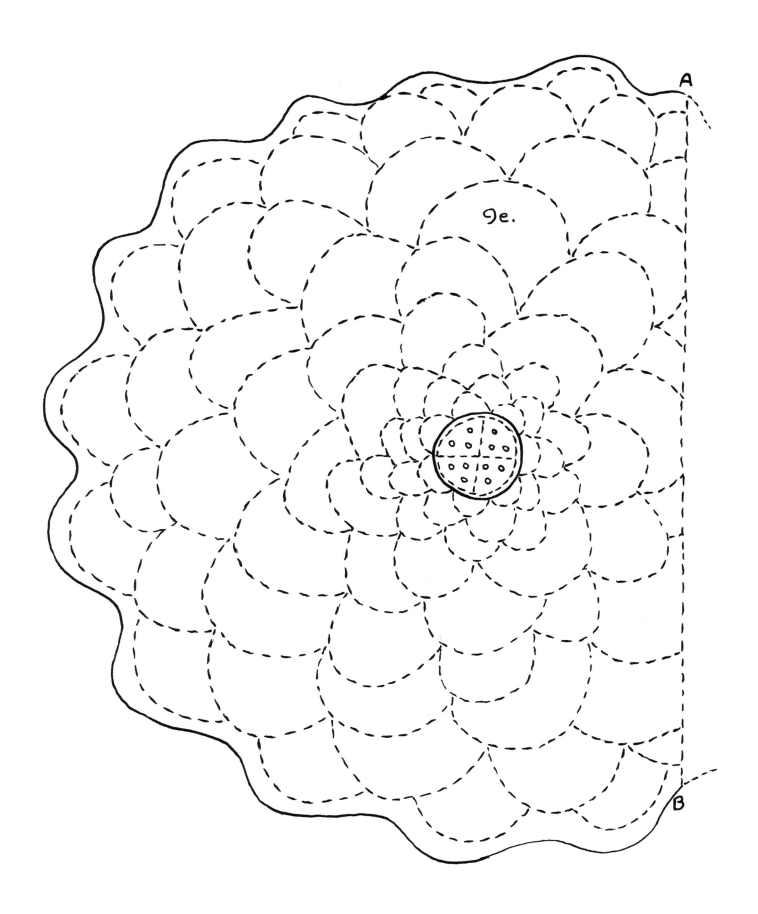

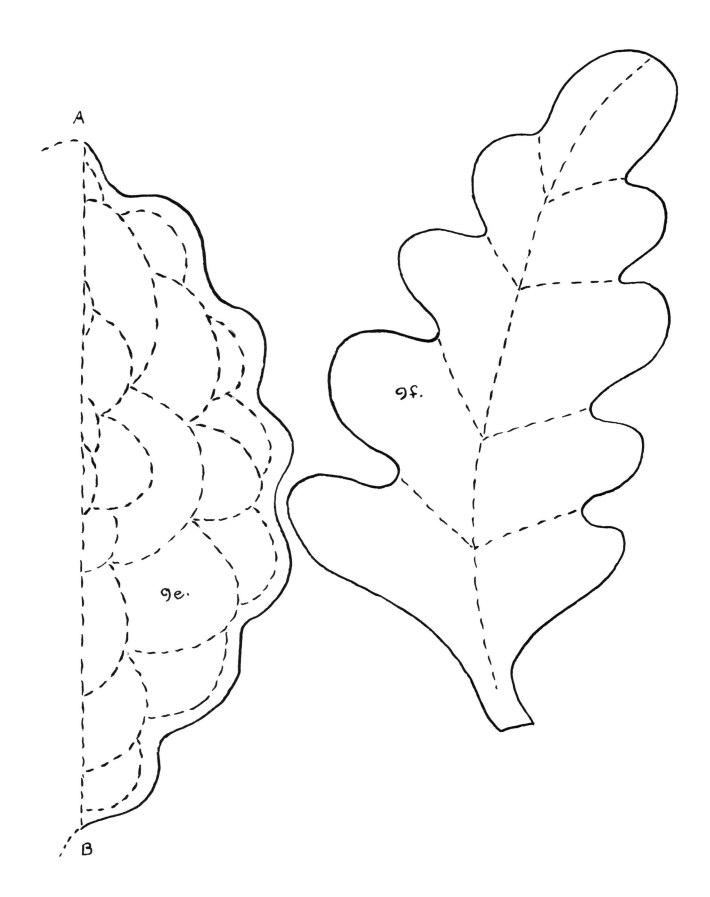

A

9e.

9f.

B

128

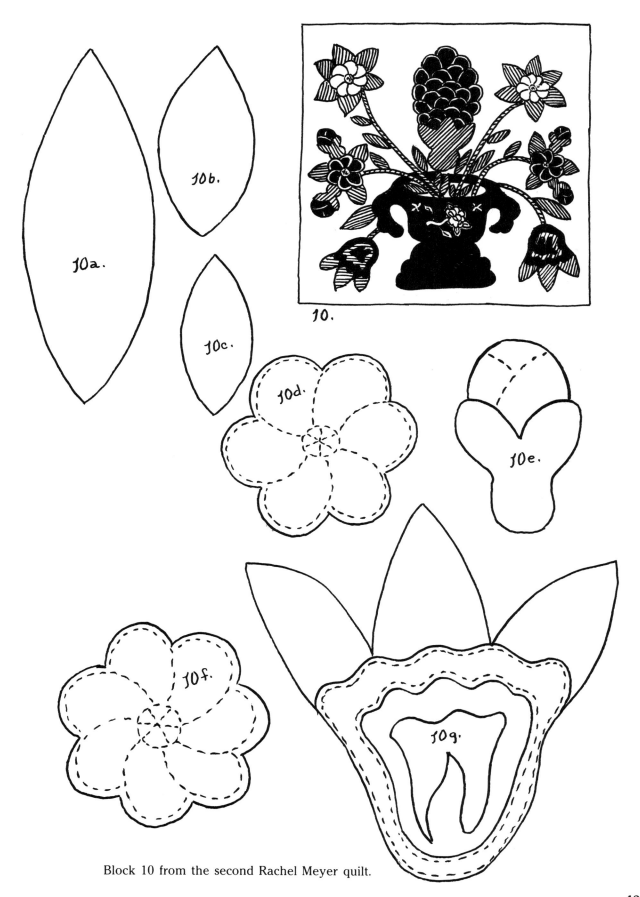

10a.

10b.

10c.

10.

10d.

10e.

10f.

10g.

Block 10 from the second Rachel Meyer quilt.

129

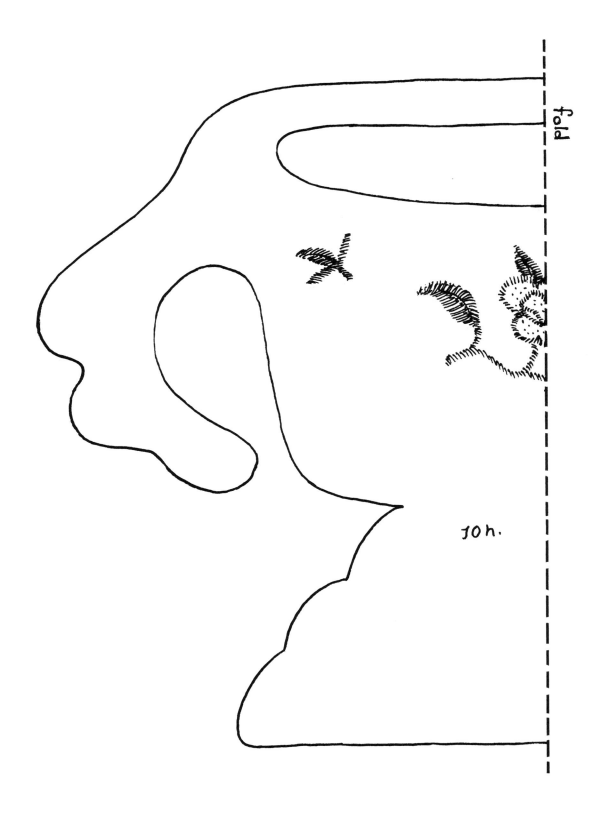

fold

10h.

130

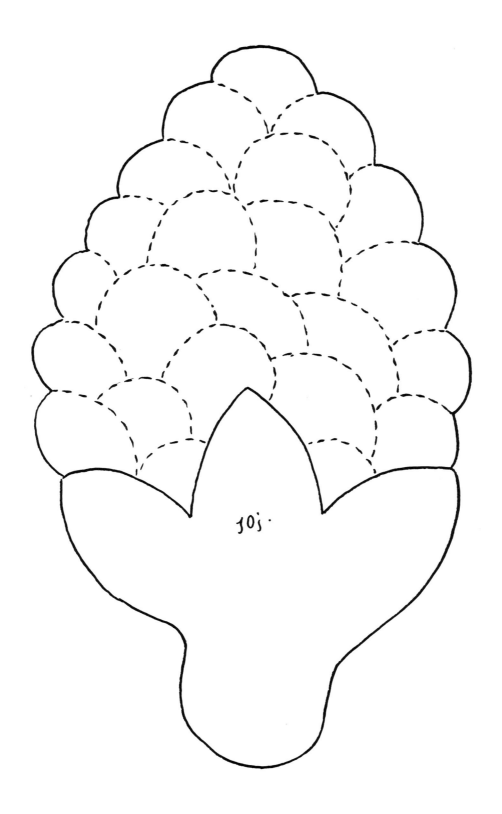

10j.

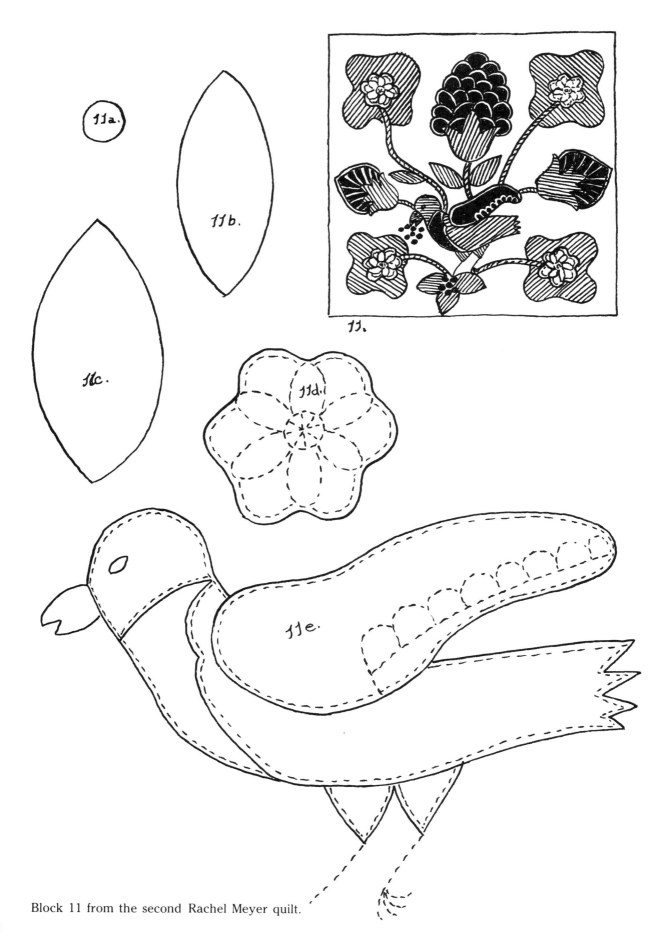

Block 11 from the second Rachel Meyer quilt.

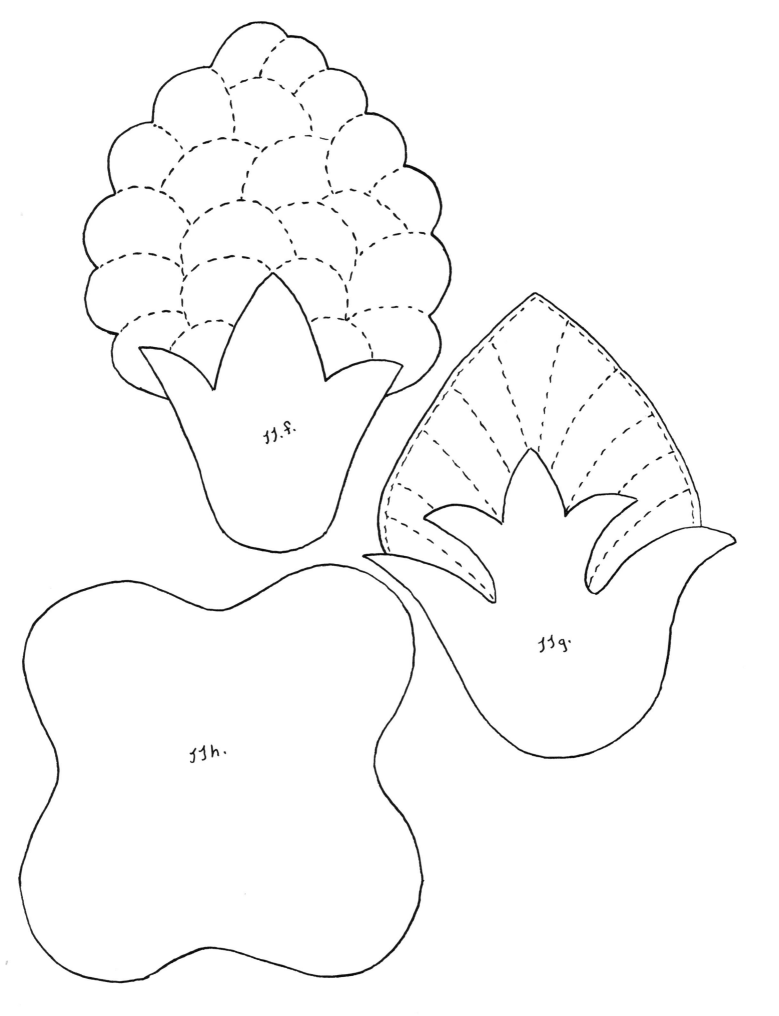

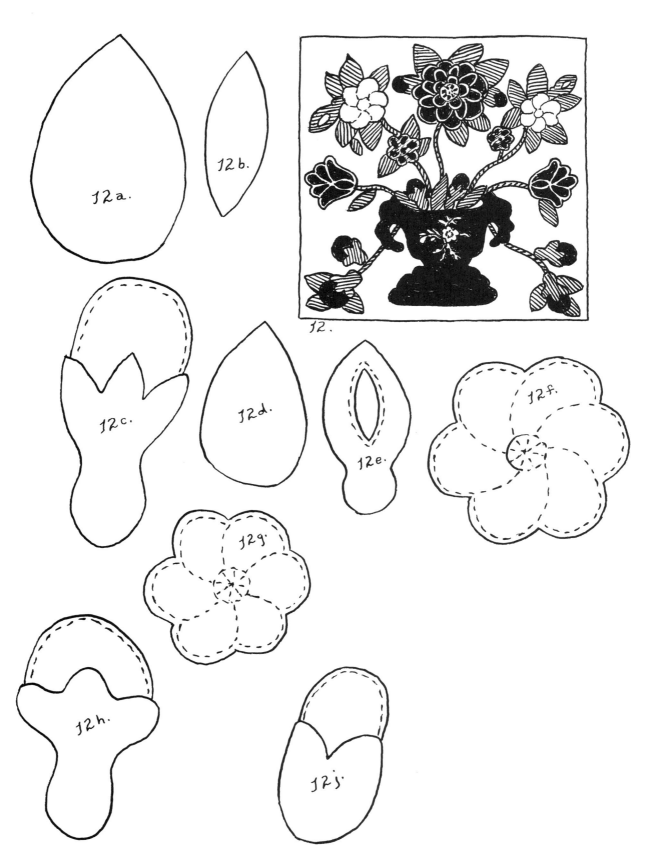

12a.

12b.

12.

12c.

12d.

12e.

12f.

12g.

12h.

12j.

Block 12 from the second Rachel Meyer quilt.

134

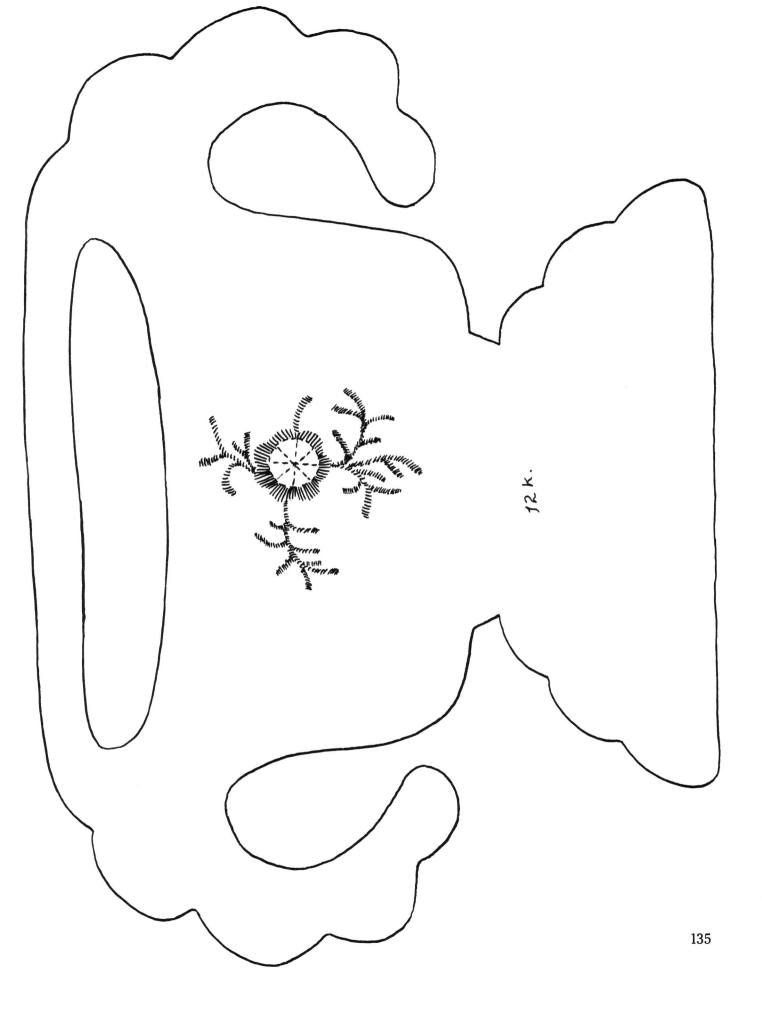

12 k.

135

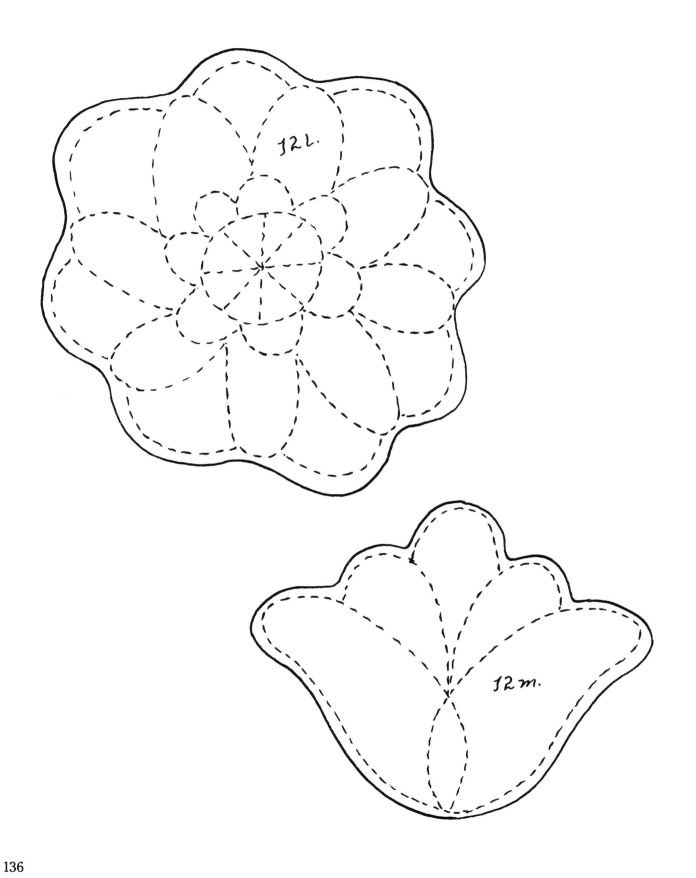

12 l.

12 m.

136

Design of the border swags from the second Rachel Meyer quilt.

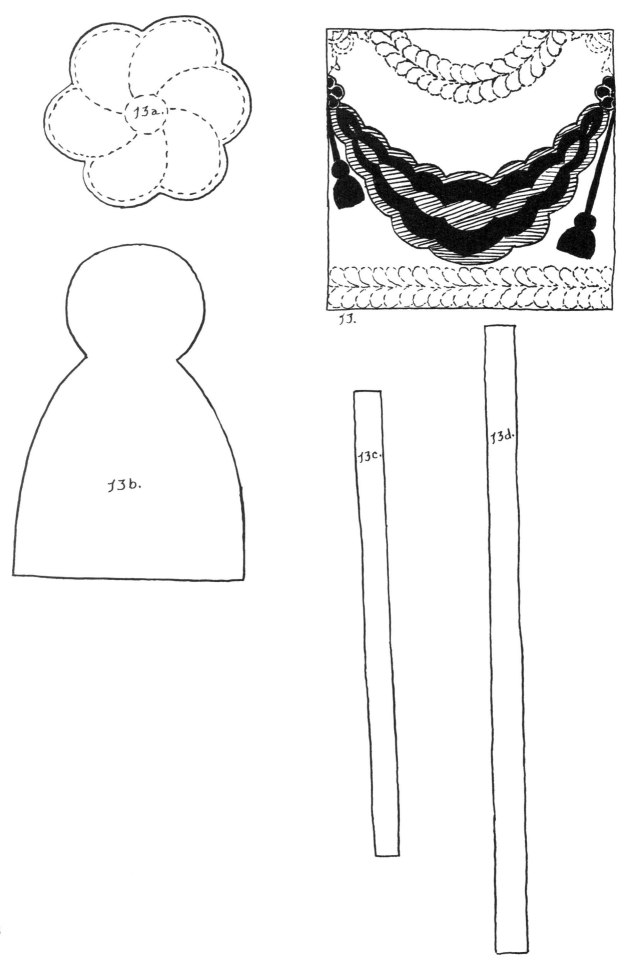

13a.

13.

13b.

13c.

13d.

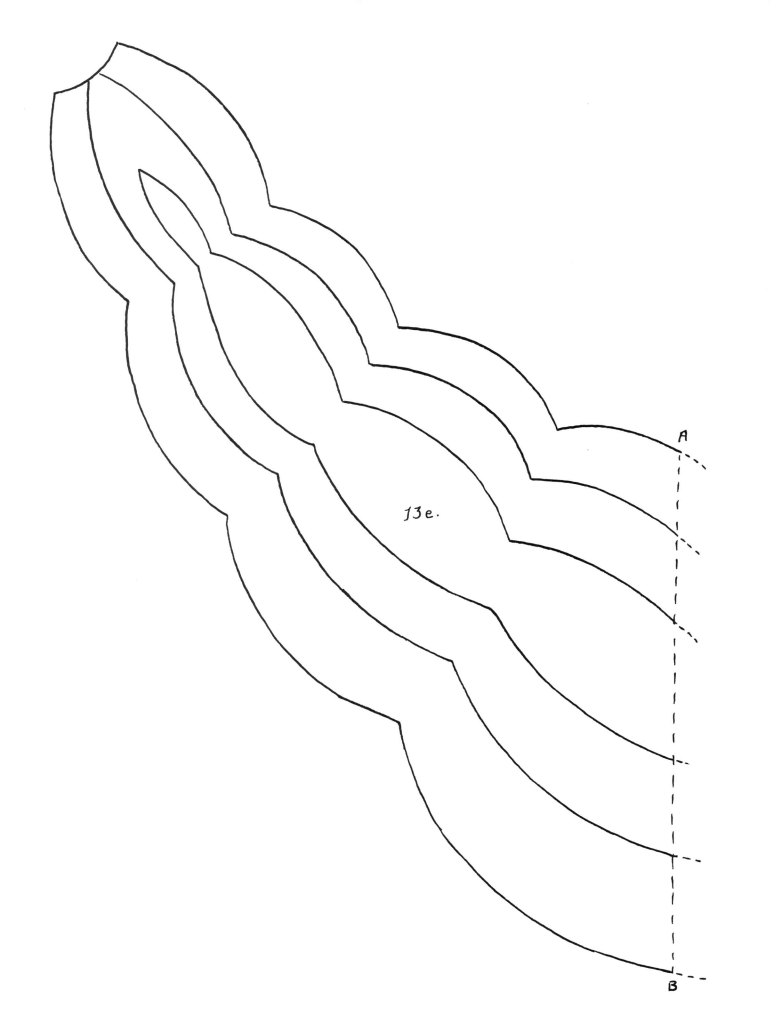

13e.

A

B

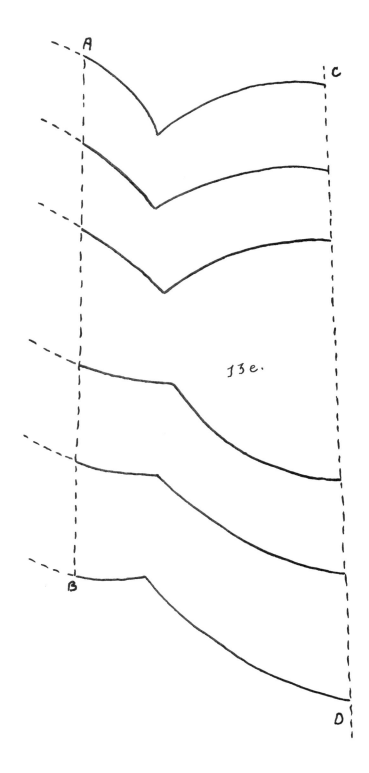

13e.

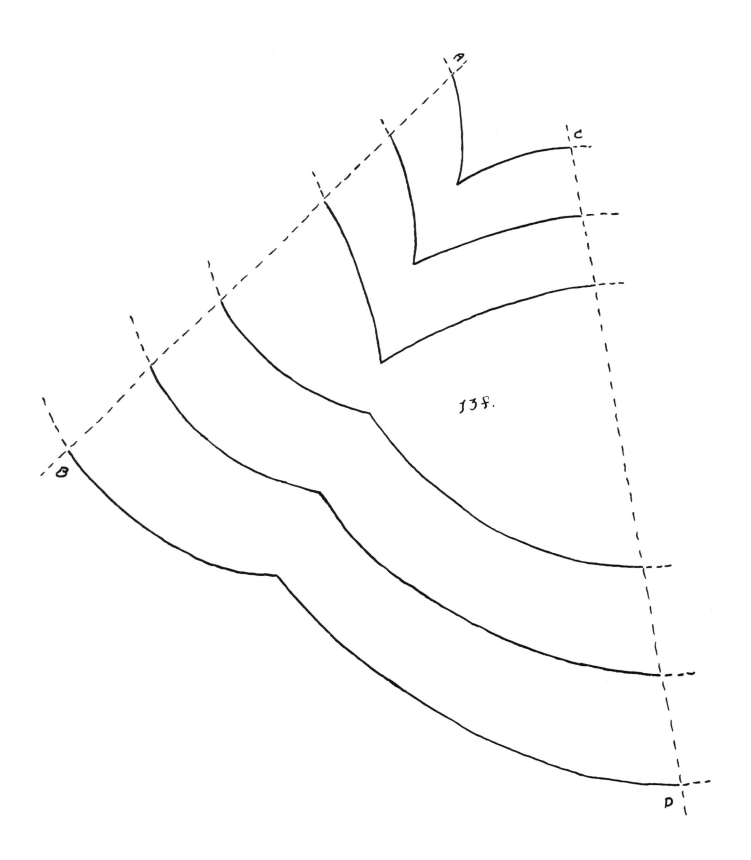

13f.

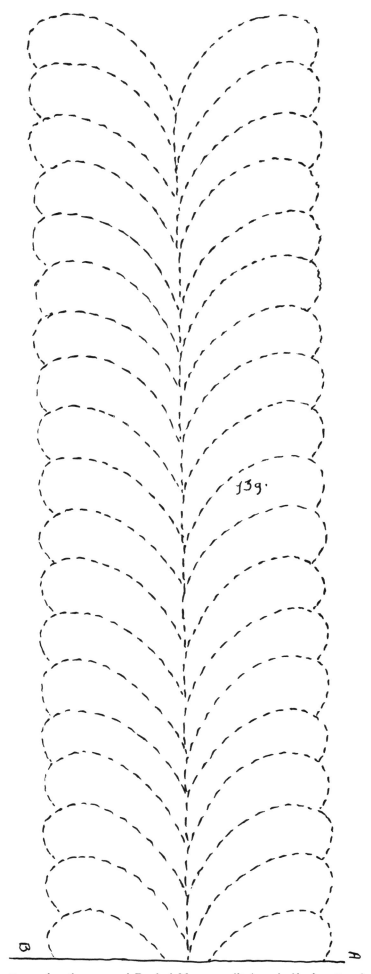

139.

B

A

Quilting patterns for the second Rachel Meyer quilt (one-half of pattern).

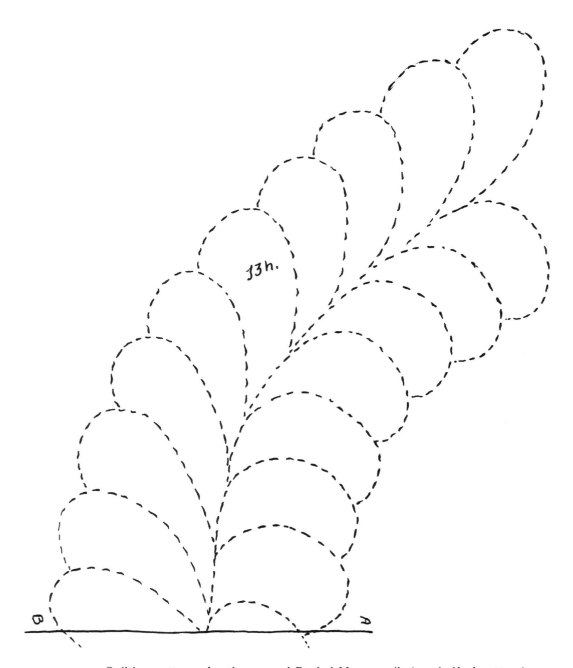

Quilting patterns for the second Rachel Meyer quilt (one-half of pattern).

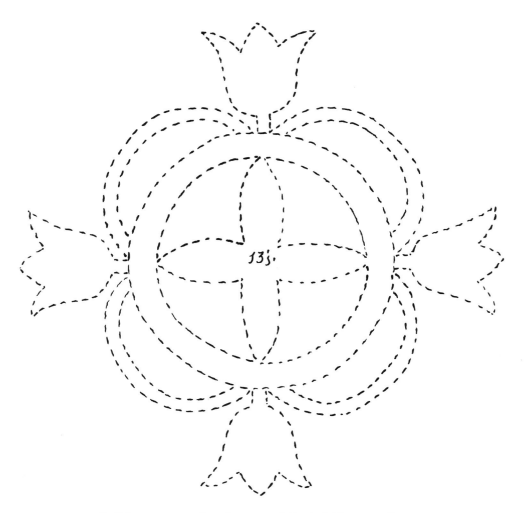

Quilting patterns for the second Rachel Meyer quilt.

4

Forerunners of the
Baltimore-Style Quilt

Most of the quilts in this section are from the 1840s and they are all the same kind of early Album or Medley quilts. Remember from the list in the first chapter that an Album quilt is made by several people, the Medley quilt by one person for herself.

There was usually a purpose in making these quilts, although the purpose differed for each quilt. You will never find two old quilts that copy one another. The copying of old quilts began in this century and has saved many old patterns that otherwise would have been lost due to the disintegration of the original quilts. In the past, however, a woman was proud of creating her own quilt and though certain patterns were extremely popular, there were differences in the details of borders and quilting or the placement of the blocks in each quilt.

The purpose of the first quilt in this section was to celebrate the campaign of William Henry Harrison, "The Log Cabin and Hard Cider" candidate for President in 1840 (See Picture 7). The log cabin symbol of the campaign appears in the middle block of the second row from the top. This is a folksy cabin with a flag on the roof, a cat on the ridge between two chimneys, hens and a cider barrel on the front lawn, and a bird building a nest in one chimney. This last has long been a symbol of happiness and prosperity. The fourth block of the third row includes the American eagle with flag which, in variation, you will see in so many of the quilts both in this book and in other quilts of the era from 1820 to 1860.

The first block in the third row, also a symbol of American freedom, is one of the many Charter Oak patterns inspired by an incident from the colonial era when the British Government threatened to revoke the Connecticut Charter. The document was hidden in an oak tree.

There are several bluebirds of happiness worked into different blocks and the first block of the first row may be meant as a lotus flower, which is a symbol of love. The next block, a heart-shaped wreath, is almost certainly a symbol of love. Whatever meanings the other blocks once had are perhaps lost to us now.

The second quilt (See Picture 8) is probably at least one decade older than the first quilt. As you can see, it has a medallion-like center with two rows of blocks around it. The border of this quilt is unusual because it frames the center medallion rather than the outer edge of the blocks. Another quilt made in the same manner is shown in Picture 16. The symbolism in this quilt includes several pineapples, representing hospitality. Baskets, vases, and wreaths of flowers or fruits, even some blocks containing both at once, are included. These were especially popular during the first half of the 19th century and were included in all of the decorative arts whose schemes could possibly work in these motifs. This quilt was made by Cinthia Arnsworth in Baltimore, Maryland.

The next quilt was made in Pennsylvania (See Picture 9). The dates given are either 1836 or 1848.

145

Picture 7 Quilt made during the 1840 Presidential Campaign. Smithsonian Institution Photo No. 35097-A.

Picture 8 Very early Baltimore-style quilt from Baltimore. By permission of the Philadelphia Museum of Art, Philadelphia, Pennsylvania.

Judging from the style of the design, I believe that the later date is correct. The information sheet also gives the following information about the quilt: "Two blocks with eagle holding flag, one block 'Texas' and one 'Lone Red Star'; obviously this quilt celebrated the independence of Texas or its admission to the Union in 1845." My opinion, after studying the quilt, is that at some time a mistake was made in copying information for this sheet, because the name 'Texas Lone Red Star' should be written as one name rather than two. This pattern is the fifth block in the second row and it reproduces the Texas state symbol almost exactly. The quilt is unusual in its number of repeat blocks. I have never seen this number of repeat blocks in any other quilt of this kind. The repeats of the eagle blocks and the fruit baskets around the center block are obviously a deliberate part of the design, since they create a balance in the center of the quilt. Except for the cornucopia block, the others do not form a design balance. I wonder if the person who started this quilt was the one who finished it. It would be interesting to study the stitches to determine whether two different hands worked on it.

The next quilt is an Autograph Presentation quilt (Picture 10) made in Maltaville, New York. Nothing more is known about it, not even the name of the person who received it at the presentation party. Each person who made a block for this quilt must have made her own favorite block since many diverse tastes are represented. They were put together tastefully to make a most harmonious whole and even the colors are balanced. The bird (possibly a phoenix) in the second row, the tulips in the next row, the cross and crown and the iris in the sixth row are all unusual designs, but the block that really intrigued me is the one in the bottom row that shows the planet Saturn with seven moons. It must have been an unusually intelligent and inquiring woman who designed and made that block. After all, in the 1840s it was unusual to find a man who was interested in astronomy, let alone a woman. Few women in those days were educated for anything but keeping a home and raising a family.

You must know the history of a quilt before labeling it a Bride's quilt. The fifth quilt in this section, (Picture 11) is a perfect example. This is a lovely, well-made quilt with good design, but there is nothing about it that would suggest that it was a Bride's quilt. Although there is a love poem in one block, it is one of those popular at the time and says nothing of weddings or marriage. The upper left-hand corner block has a scroll drawn in its center with the words "E. J. Bailey Commenced June, 1850." The poem, inked in Spencerian script with many scrolls in the lettering, appears in the center block of the first row. The poem says

> Sweet Flower,[2] bright as an Indian sky
>   Yet mild as Beautysoft blue eye;
> Tho Charm be Unassuming shed
>   a modest Splendoure o're the Mead.

The last wreath in the bottom row also has a scroll inked in the center, which says, "Finished October 30, 1851." The history with this quilt gives the information that the quilt was made by Eliza Jane Bailey, born Feb. 13, 1832. She married Levi Manahan on Oct. 30, 1851, which is the last date given in the bottom block of the quilt. According to family history, this lovely quilt was used on the marriage bed of Eliza and Levi. The strawberries in the border are padded.

The names on the sixth quilt suggest that this is an Album quilt (*See* Picture 12). The quilt was in New York City when the original drawing was made for The Index of American Design, but it could have been made in any state from Virginia to New York. I would guess, however, that this quilt was made in Maryland. The center basket, the roses in the spray just under it, and the vase in the last block of the fourth row are all repeated in a more refined design in the Baltimore style quilts of the following decade. I did not receive an information sheet with this photo and so, unfortunately, both the names on the quilt, the date it was made, and all of the other information seems to have been lost. Only the name of the watercolor artist is plain enough to be read. I cannot tell you anything more about this quilt except that it is very pleasing.

[2]These first two words are faded in the original quilt and can only be guessed at.

Picture 9 Quilt made in Pennsylvania, 1835-1845. By permission of the Index of American Design, National Gallery of Art (Photo NYC-Te-151), Washington, D.C.

Picture 10 Autograph Presentation quilt from Maltaville, New York. By permission of the Smithsonian Institution, Washington, D.C.

The seventh quilt in this chapter (Picture 13) is from Pennsylvania and is so typically a Pennsylvania Dutch design that it almost speaks to us in dialect. It is a charming quilt which foreshadows the folk designs that were to take over this form of quilt designing before the end of the 19th century. If you look at the motifs with people and animals that appear between the blocks, you will find them very similar to the other block designs in this chapter. Individual flowers, birds, and leaves reproduce so ex-

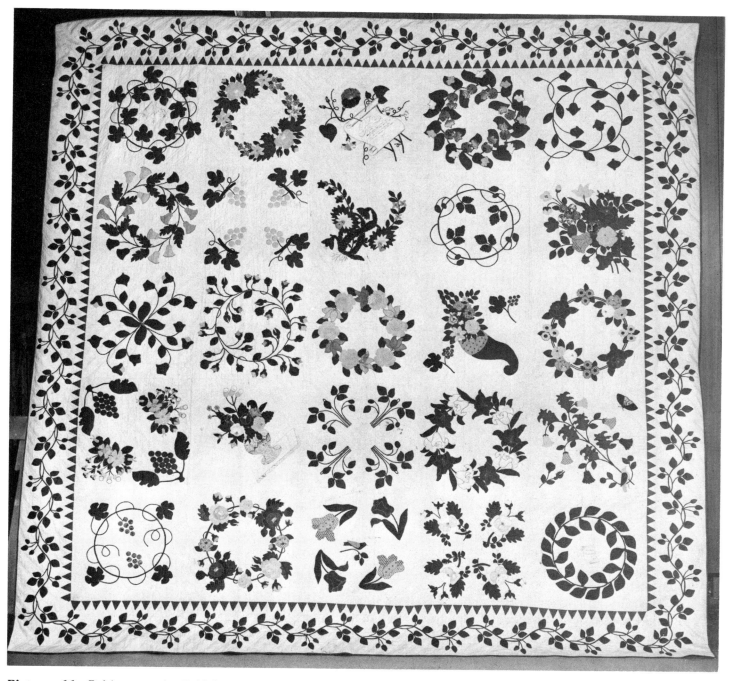

Picture 11 Baltimore-style Bride's quilt, 1850-1851. Smithsonian Institution Photo No. P63342.

actly the motifs of the other quilts in this section that their common inspiration is quite plain.

Picture 14 shows a quilt design which was made 20 years later than the others in this chapter, but which is otherwise so similar that it must be included

here. It has the same eagle and flag as the others and could also be compared with the eagle and flag designs in the next chapter. The only real difference between this quilt and earlier ones is that the blocks are much more crowded. This crowding and multi-

Picture 12 Album quilt found in New York City. By permission of the Index of American Design, National Gallery of Art (Photo NYC-Te-177), Washington, D.C.

plication of elements in a single design can also be found in the designs offered in women's magazines. This quilt was made in Maryland and is eight feet ten inches square.

The ninth quilt (Picture 15) is made of chintz and is different from the others in this book although the technique involved is used in one or two blocks of several of the other quilts. Chintz of many different printed patterns and colors was used for each of the blocks. The printed motifs are cut out around their outlines and then appliquéd either as they appeared or combined in other patterns. The blocks are in alternating shades of blue and green, and pink and green. The lattice strips between the blocks and the narrow border are blue with a printed Greek Key pattern. Because the designs are printed in the material, they are still bright and clear. Many quilts of this kind were made and some are on display in museums. I believe they can be grouped with the American graphic quilts in inspiration when, as in the one pictured, each block was made differently. Some chintz quilts were made like the Medallion quilts and others are like bedspreads in an all-over design. Most quilts of all three kinds were made from French chintzes and imply the makers' affluence because the materials were quite expensive. However, some were made by cutting up the muslin bedspreads printed with chintz-like patterns manufactured by John Hewson in Philadelphia. Hewson began his industry before the Revolutionary War and continued it for an unknown period after the war. He was a soldier and patriot who was captured during the war but managed to escape. Judging from the small number of authentic Hewson spreads and the even fewer quilts proven to have been made using these spreads, it is impossible to tell whether Mr.

152

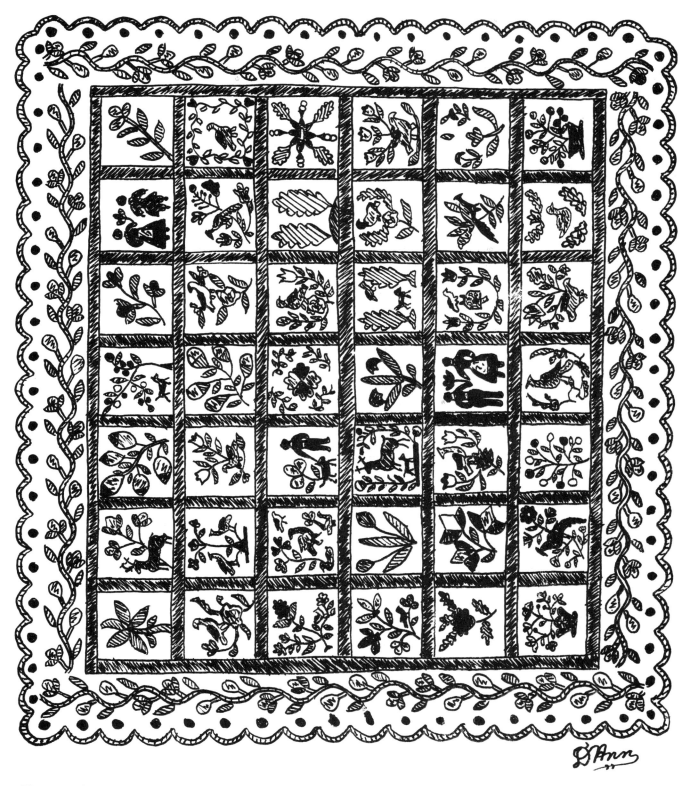

Picture 13 Large Medley quilt from Pennsylvania. By permission of the Index of American Design, National Gallery of Art, Washington, D.C.

Picture 14   Album quilt from Maryland, 1860s. Smithsonian Institution Photo No. 75145.

154

Picture 15 Chintz Friendship quilt from Baltimore, 1844. Courtesy of the St. Louis Art Museum, St. Louis, Missouri.

Picture 16 Baltimore-style Bride's quilt, 1820-1840.

Hewson's business was started to imitate the chintz quilts or the quilts were imitating the spreads. The small number of these quilts in the museums and in the antique markets proves that this was a short-lived though beautiful fad. To continue our appraisal of the chintz quilt top pictured here, there are two kinds of blocks in this quilt: those made from a whole design appliquéd intact to a block and those cut out in small details and appliquéd in a pieced-together design to the block. This quilt is listed as a Friendship quilt made in Baltimore in 1844. It is a top which was unfinished. You can see the delicacy of design and color in this quilt. Although it is a shame that it was never finished with backing and quilting, this deficiency may have ensured the quilt top's present good condition.

The last drawing (Picture 16) shows a group of women at a quilt exhibition. I have copied a newspaper photo and concentrated on making the quilt clear. The ladies are only sketched and I assure all my readers that it was a lovely group of women who look nothing like the drawing. They are examining a Maryland quilt that was taken to Iowa as the marriage quilt of a pioneer family. According to its history, this quilt was probably made in the 1820-1840 period, it is my guess from its design and appearance that it was made earlier in this period rather than later. It has a modified Medallion center with a border. This quilt differs from the similar quilt in this chapter (Picture 8) by also having an outside border. The baskets are made from strips of cloth that seem to be characteristic of Maryland quilts of the early 19th century, no matter what other motifs were used in them. The rose in the border of this quilt is an interesting variation of the common quilter's rose. The block shown separately is an Odd Fellows Block with several symbols of that organization. It gives the maker's maiden name, Ellen Carr, and has the words "Love, Friendship, Truth" embroidered around the "Heart in Hand" symbol in the center of the block. This quilt is now owned by Ellen Carr's descendants in Iowa.

I think if you study the individual blocks and their design parts, you will agree that these quilts are all individual interpretations of a basic design inspiration. They reflect the training and economic circumstances of the individuals who made them. Groups of quilters would have shared similar backgrounds, so this premise holds true for them also. It would be interesting for the reader to look up specific blocks from these quilts in a good comprehensive quilt block collection to see just how many of these alone are used, in multiples, to make quilt tops. Charter Oak is represented in several forms among these blocks. Lotus Flower, President's Wreath, and several others are all included here. It is within the scope of neither this chapter nor this book to explore whether individual block quilts or the American graphic quilts are older. It is my guess that the single-block motif quilts were made first and that favorite blocks were then taken and used in graphic quilt tops by women who were unsure of their imagination when a pretty block was needed for an Album or Presentation quilt. The more self-confident or skillful women made individual block patterns for each quilt they worked on. Judging from the silly blocks that were included in some of the quilts, I wonder why more women did not copy the traditional patterns.

5

A True Baltimore-Style Presentation Quilt

This quilt, Picture 17, which was presented to a naval captain, is a classic Baltimore-style quilt. It has all the typical motifs and ingredients, is signed by the makers, and even has the typical color scheme. The main block has the dedication, "Presented to Capt. George W. Rufsell by His Friends of Baltimore August 23rd 1852." The records of the Port of Baltimore reveal that there were many captains with the last name of Russell (the f written in the name of the inscription is the old style of s; I do not know why two different styles of letters were used together). In the records, this particular George Russell does not stand out but he must have done something remarkable to have prompted his friends to make this beautiful quilt for him.

The names of 22 women are stamped in ornamental letters on the blocks and borders of the quilt. Several were probably related because they have the same last names. One lady was unusual in that she signed two blocks.

In looking over the stitches of the quilting, I was able to determine that at least sixteen women helped in the quilting. There is evidence that seven women did the quilting in the areas needing fancy patterns and one woman, who was the best needlewoman, did the entire center. One person had marked the quilting pattern for the entire top before the quilting and she did a very good job. The pattern is even and well-balanced over the entire quilt top. I could not find any mistakes in the marking. She turned the corners with the feathers perfectly. To give you the information on each of the pattern motifs, I have sketched each block and sections from the four borders. See the back cover of this book, which illustrates the colors used for each motif.

All the material used in the appliqué is cotton and the blocks are each 17-½-inches square. The names were put on the squares with small stamps, which was the usual practice in the eastern part of our country in the mid-19th century. Each quilter had her own stamp with her name so she could mark her work. The name was usually in rather ornate script and had some decoration, often willow branches, delicately swirled around it. A lady's stamp was kept with her other sewing tools in her sewing basket. Some of the blocks had more inkwork added to the appliqué; this was done by hand with a pen. This inkwork included the tendrils of the grapes, leaf veining, and some stems on the smaller fruit and flowers. The ink has faded to brown with time.

Picture 19 shows a rather unique block. The motif is a small steamboat in a flower wreath. It may be that this ship is modeled on Capt. Russell's ship. I have not been able to find a ship exactly like this one but the details are so well done that I cannot believe they were invented by the needlewoman. There is an exposed walking beam above the wheelhousing and this wooden ship has two smokestacks and no masts for the sails that were always carried in addition to the steam boilers during this period. These two features make the design unique. I have combed all available books trying to find a similar ship but I have been unsuccessful so far. I am hoping one of my readers with a wider knowledge of ships than mine will be able to place this example and inform me.

Fortunately, the date of this quilt is given in the inscription along with the names of the quilt makers. It is wonderful to have so much definite information about this quilt's origin, as it is a rare quilt that includes so much documentation inscribed indelibly

Picture 17 Baltimore-style Presentation quilt, the Captain Russell quilt, 1852. The Baltimore Museum of Art: The Hooper, Strauss, Pell, and Kent Funds.

Picture 18 Fruit cornucopia, block 1 from the Captain Russell Quilt, by Susan DeFord.

160

Picture 19 Steamboat in a wreath, block 2 from the Captain Russell quilt, by Elizabeth A. George.

Picture 20 Odd Fellows symbols in a wreath, block 3 from the Captain Russell quilt, by Susan Brashears.

162

Picture 21 Flower cornucopia with birds, block 4 from the Captain Russell quilt, by Mary J. Atchisson.

Picture 22   Fruit basket in a wreath, block 5 from the Captain Russell quilt, by Zorah M. Coy.

Picture 23 Ornamental anchor in a wreath, block 6 from the Captain Russell quilt, by Sophia Coy.

Picture 24 Flower cornucopia with bird and butterfly, block 7 from the Captain Russell quilt, by Edmonia Brashears.

Picture 25 Flower basket in a wreath, block 8 from the Captain Russell quilt, by Susan Brashears.

Picture 26 Flower nosegay in a wreath, block 9 from the Captain Russell quilt, by Rachel A. Russell.

168

Picture 27 Flower cornucopia with pineapple, block 10 from the Captain Russell quilt, by Mary A. Russell.

Picture 28 Flower basket in a wreath, block 11 from the Captain Russell quilt, by Mary Ellen Russell.

170

Picture 29 Ornamental bird in a wreath, block 12 from the Captain Russell quilt, by Carrie H. W. Ruff.

171

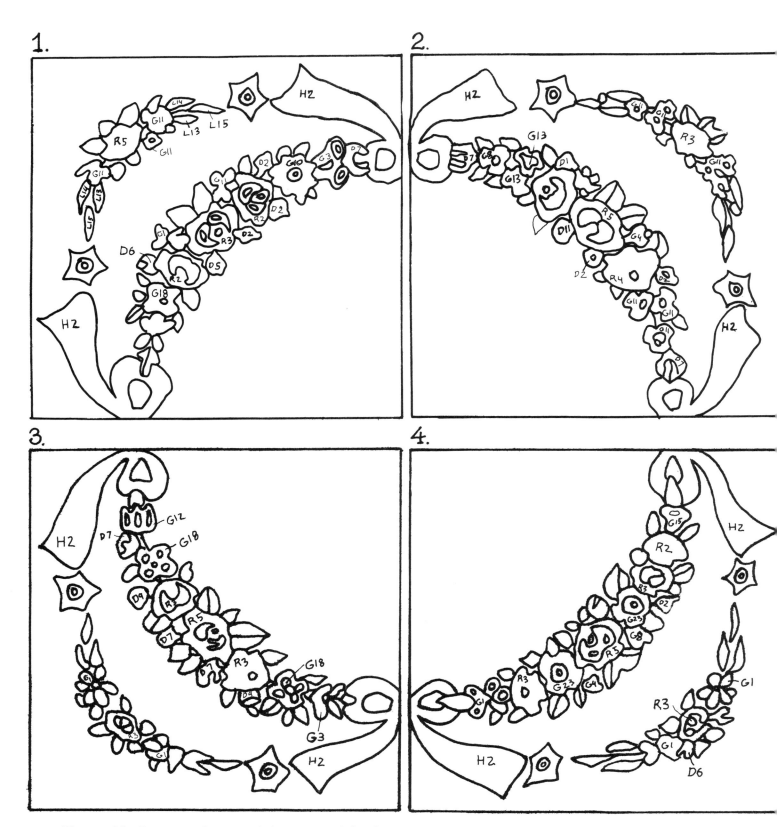

Picture 30 Four wreaths around the center of the Captain Russell quilt, by Agnes E.
German, Kate Bond, Mary Bond, and Martha Winchester.

Picture 31 Eagle and flag, center of the Captain Russell quilt, by Sarah H. George.

Picture 32 Sections from the four borders of the Captain Russell quilt. First border by Sarah Mann; second border by Susan Craft; third border by Virginia Joyce, Mary E. George, and Mary A. Joyce; fourth border by Rosabal Pawley.

Block 2 from the Captain Russell quilt.

on its top. There is some mystery, however, about the subsequent history of the quilt. The former owner, Mr. Leo F. Bowers of Baltimore, has found in the naval records of that city that a Captain George F. Russell commanded a vessel for the Union side during the Civil War in the 1860s. Also found was the record of a ship called the *North Carolina,* 115 tons, built in Fayetteville, North Carolina, in 1817 and registered as an American Merchant vessel. On the wheelhousing of the ship on the quilt is an inscription in ink, partly worn away, which may have carried the words *North Carolina.* These facts cannot be further connected but they serve to confirm some of the information on the quilt.

Mr. Bowers' family has a long history in the city of Baltimore. He obtained the quilt some years ago as part of a legacy of family treasures bequeathed by a quite elderly great-aunt. Mr. Bowers, being something of an antiquarian, immediately began to

research the family history for the names on the quilt, but found that as far as the records are concerned, none of the ladies whose names are on the quilt are related to his family. The quilt had been given to Mr. Bowers' great-aunt, according to a statement by her some years ago, by a relative from a still earlier generation. Thus, the quilt has been held in this one family in Baltimore for 100 years or more. How it left the possession of the Russell family and passed into that of the Bowers family is lost to us. We must all be grateful to Mr. Bowers who originally allowed inclusion of this lovely example in our study. The quilt is now in the Baltimore Museum of Art.

The needlewomen of the 1850s did not use exact patterns for these lovely quilts. Instead they memorized the shapes of flowers, buds, and leaves; cut these shapes from their cloth, free-hand; and appliquéd them in place. The above motif and those following (pages 176–201) have been accurately

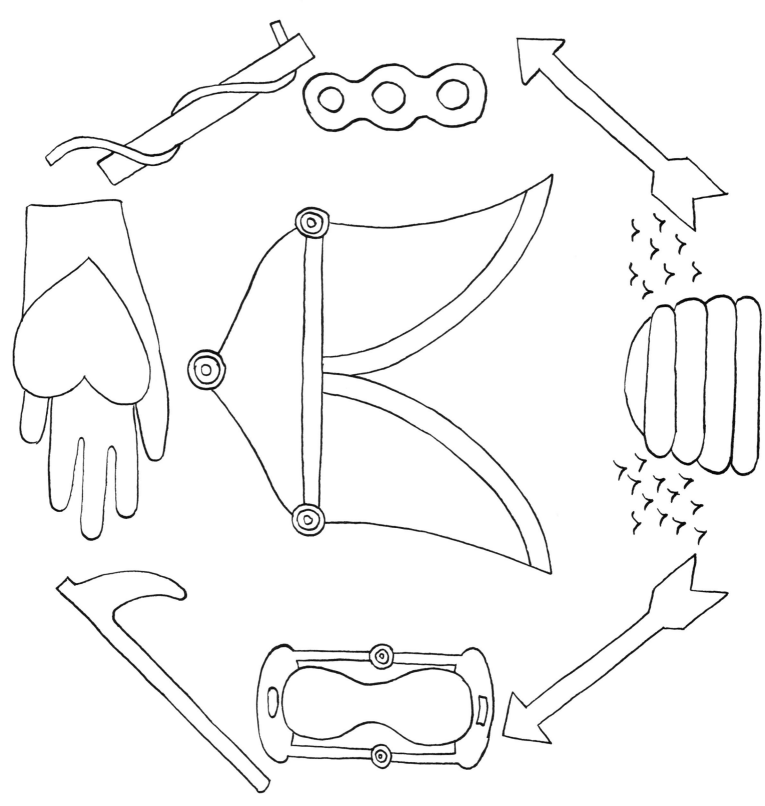

Block 3 from the Captain Russell quilt.

Block 5 from the Captain Russell quilt.

Block 6 from the Captain Russell quilt.

Block 8 from the Captain Russell quilt.

Block 9 from the Captain Russell quilt.

Block 11 from the Captain Russell quilt.

Block 12 from the Captain Russell quilt.

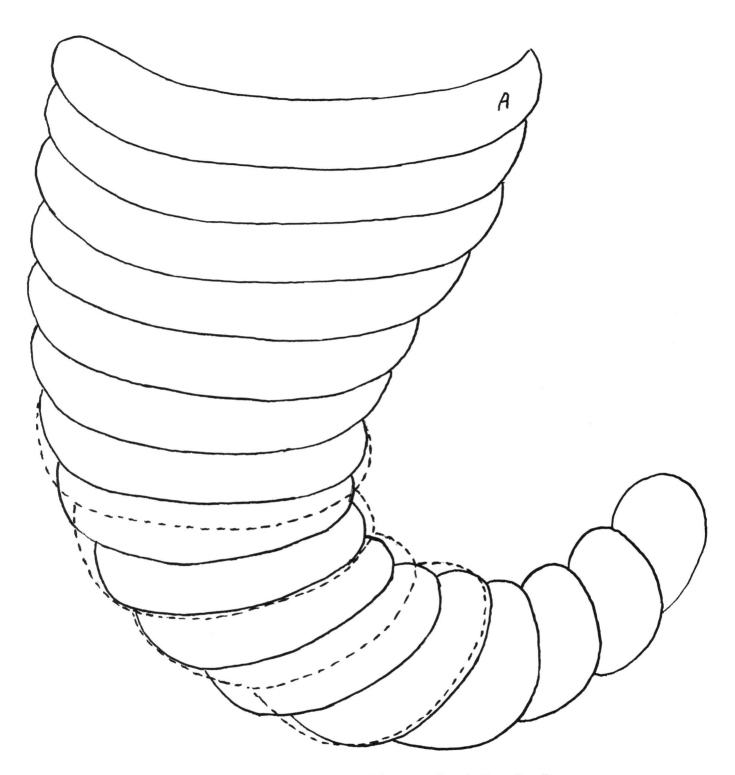

Cornucopia pattern for blocks 1, 4, 7, and 10 from the Captain Russell quilt.

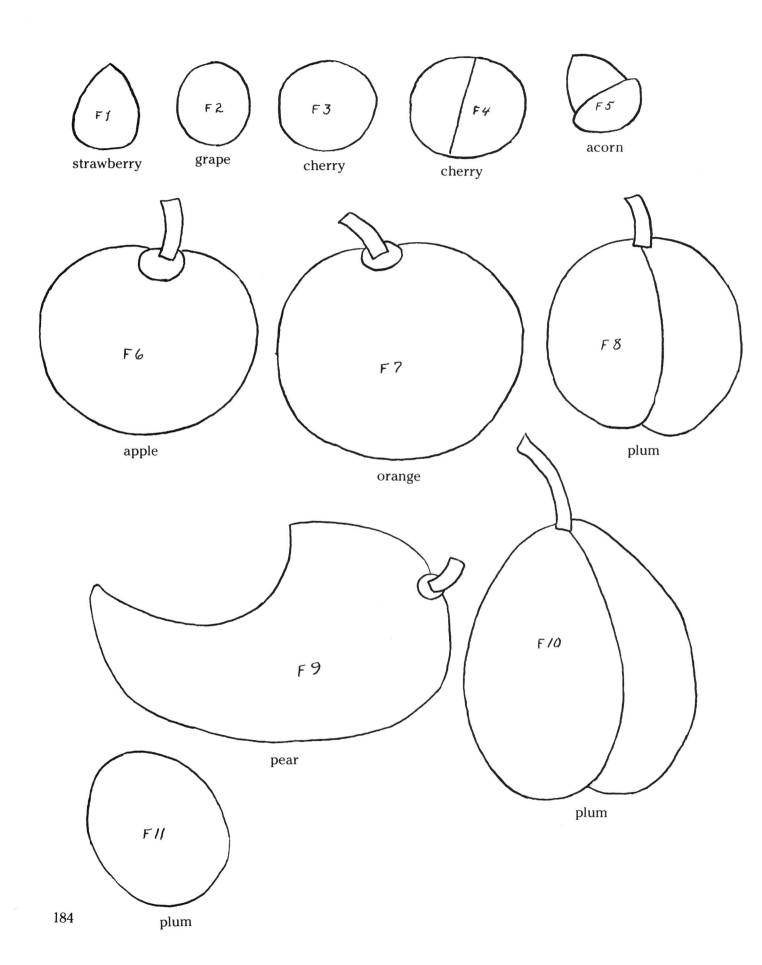

F 1 strawberry

F 2 grape

F 3 cherry

F 4 cherry

F 5 acorn

F 6 apple

F 7 orange

F 8 plum

F 9 pear

F 10 plum

F 11 plum

184

E1

E2

A

B

A

B

185

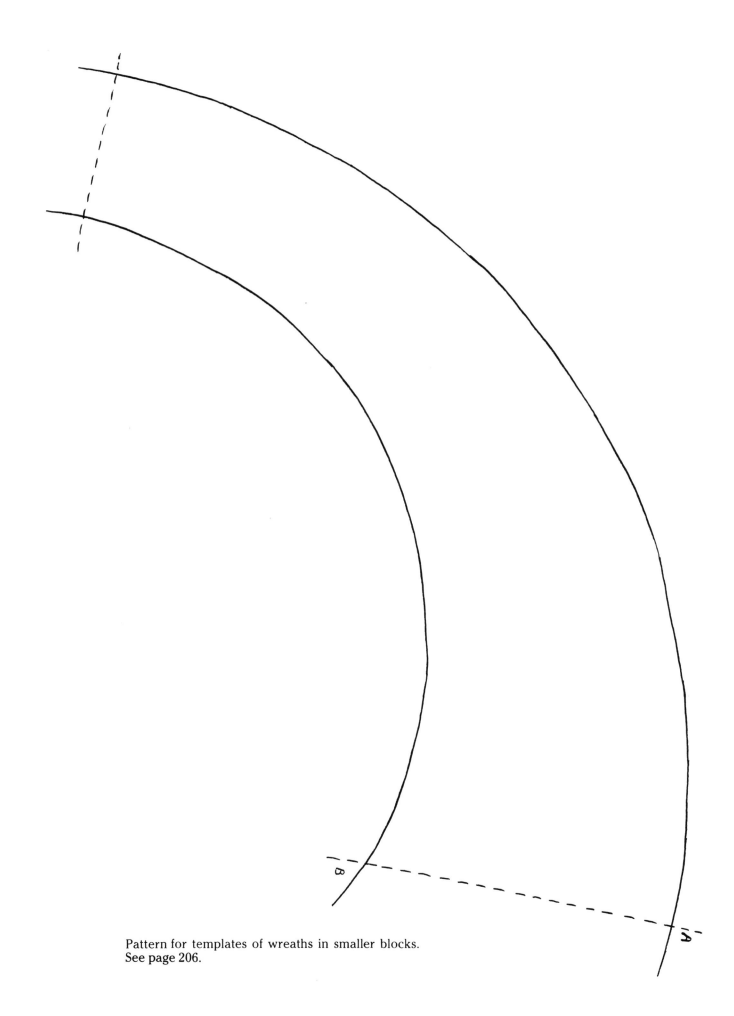

Pattern for templates of wreaths in smaller blocks.
See page 206.

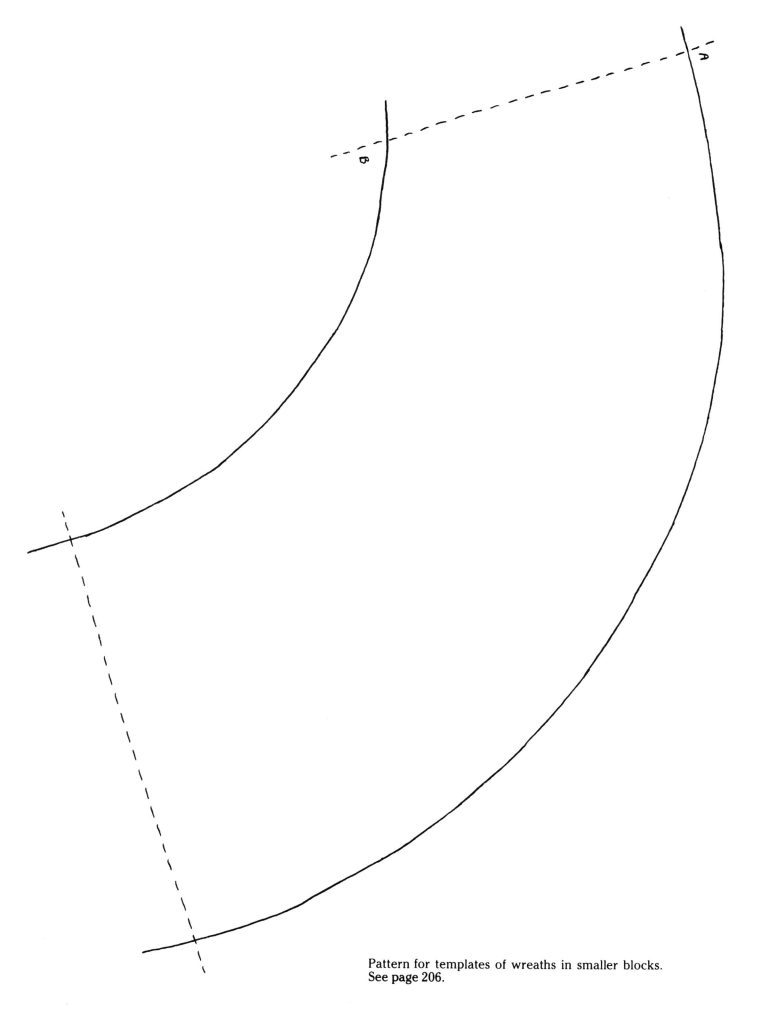

Pattern for templates of wreaths in smaller blocks.
See page 206.

1C

2C

3C

B1

B2

B3

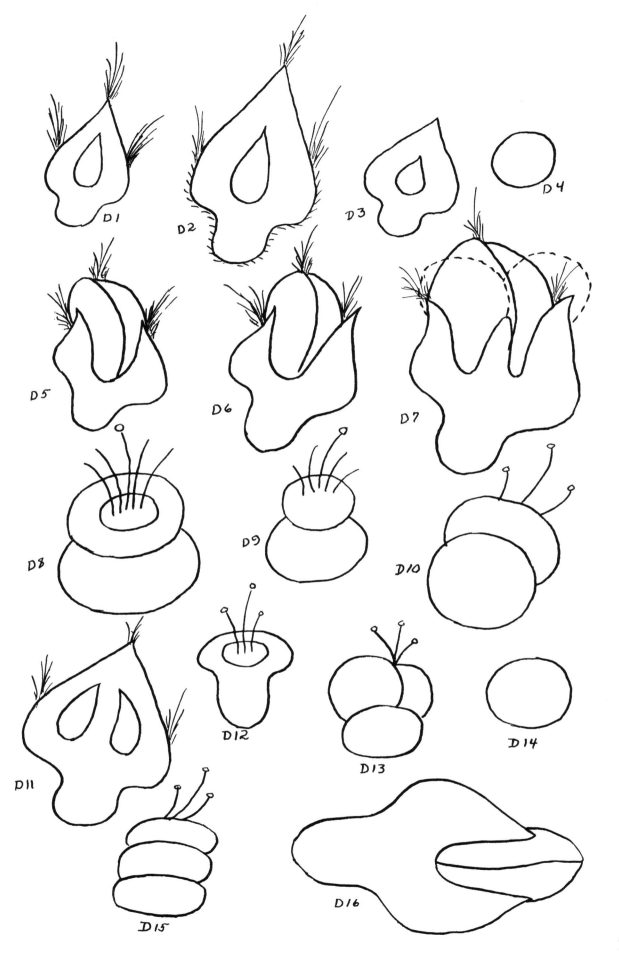

189

G13

G14

G15

G16

G17

G20

G18

G19

G21

G22

190

G1

G2

G3

G4

G5

G6

G7

G8

G9

G10

G11

G12

192

193

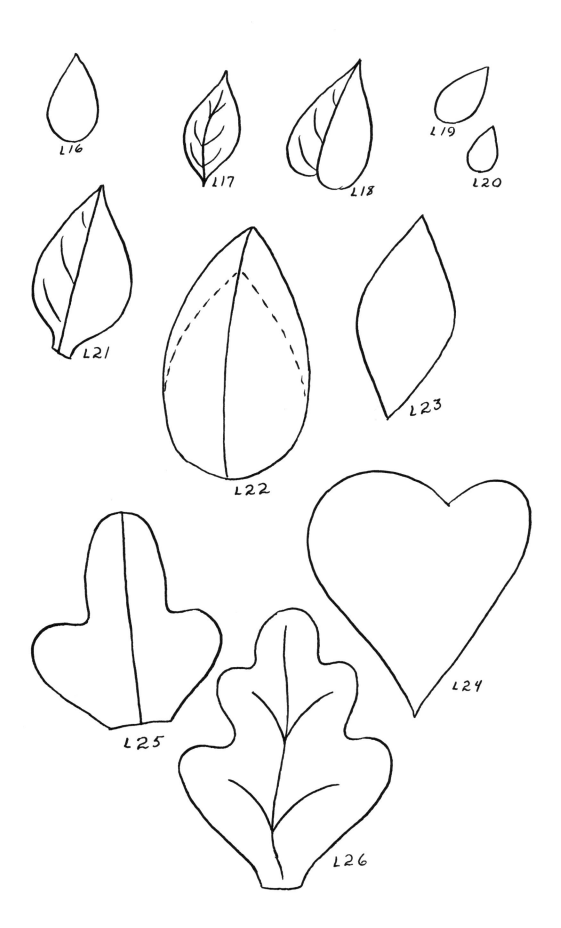

L16

L17

L18

L19

L20

L21

L22

L23

L24

L25

L26

194

R1

R2

R3

R4

R5

195

Center block from the Captain Russell quilt.

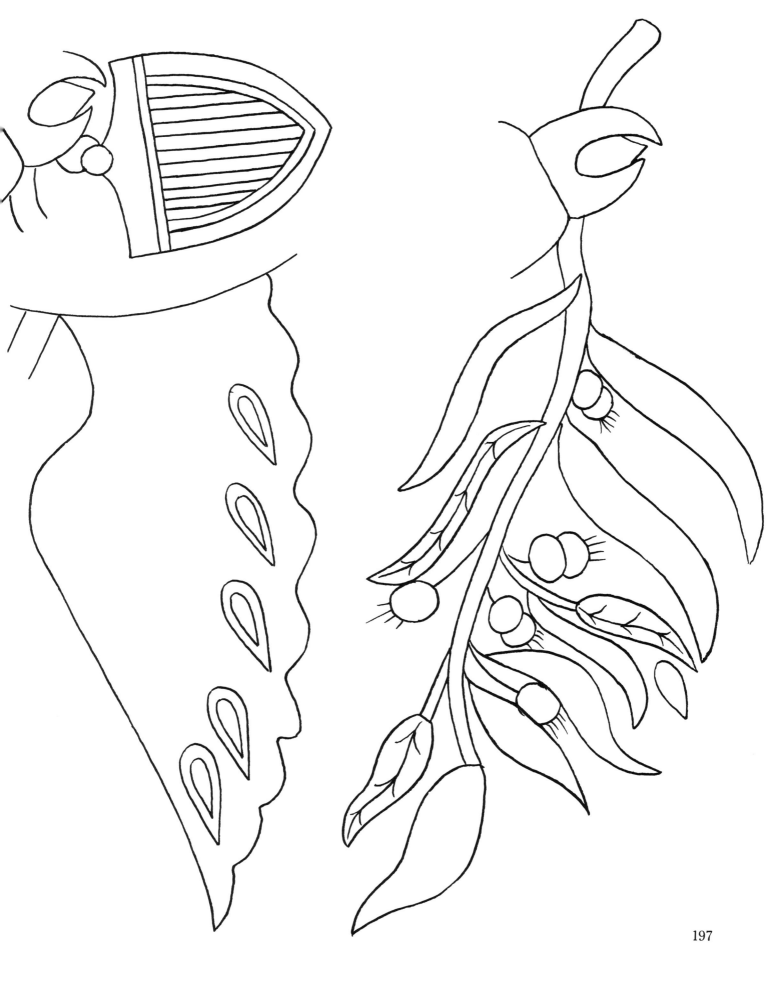

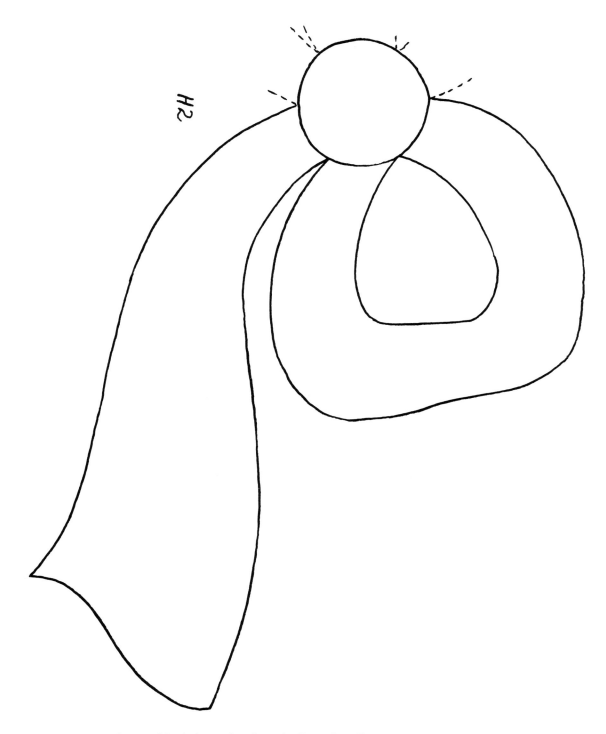

H2

Center block from the Captain Russell quilt.

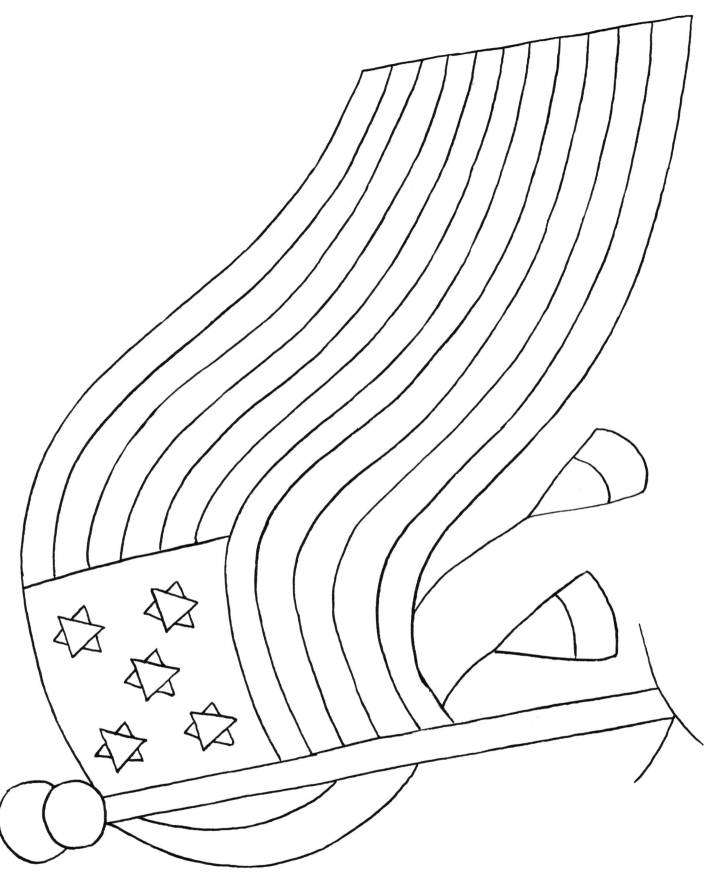

Pattern for ribbon bows in the center block.

199

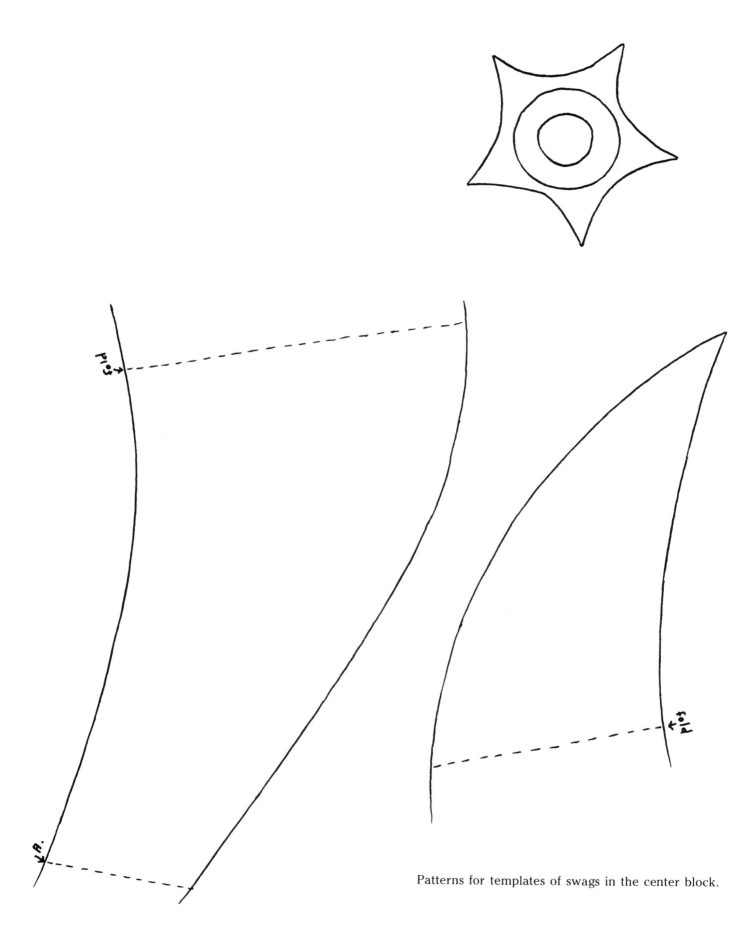

Patterns for templates of swags in the center block.

Quilting Designs for Captain Russell Quilt

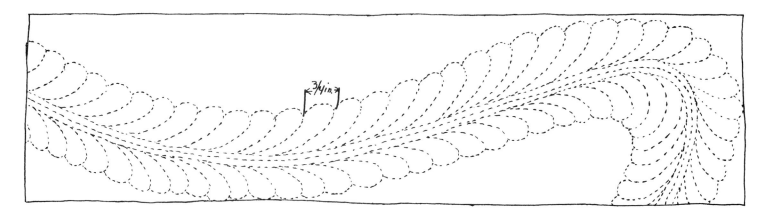

1. This design was used between the center block and the outer row of blocks and the border.

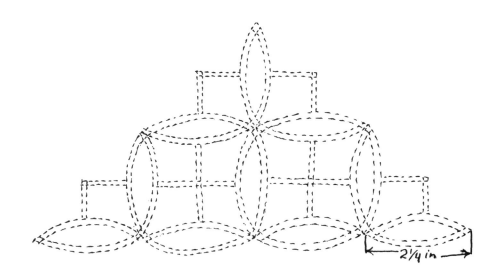

2. Used as a fill-in between the top two sections of the large swags and small swags on the center block. Also used as a quilted fill-in between the edges of the circular appliqué designs on the row of blocks and the corners of those blocks. Each of the ovals is about 2¼ inches long and 1½ inches wide.

3. This device is used only under the wings of the eagle on the center block.

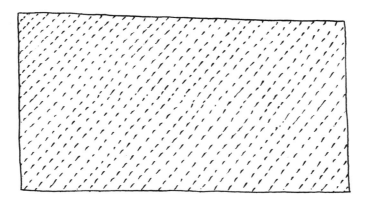

4. Background filler for the entire quilt.

Q J.

measured and drawn for use as a pattern; however, this method did not work as well for the leaves, smaller buds, and flowers. I measured and drew representative shapes of all that were used in the quilt, but since they had been used in almost every block and cut free-hand, there were no two the same size anywhere on the quilt.

To make a duplicate quilt, begin with the blocks made up of appliquéd wreaths and center designs (blocks 2, 3, 5, 6, 8, 9, 10, 11, and the center block).

On pages 186–187 are the patterns for one-half of the template for the wreaths in the smaller blocks. Trace these patterns on tissue paper to form one

ring. Then pencil the ring's outline lightly on the cloth square.

The template patterns for the large and small swags in the center block are on page 200. The "A" on the larger pattern indicates where the edge of the ribbon bow is overlaid by the appliqué pieces in the large swags.

Cut out the roses and other large motifs for the wreaths (pages 188, 190–92, 195) and place them on the squares within the penciled outlines for the wreath swags (see the appropriate block drawings on pages 161, 162, 164, 165, 167, 168, and 170–172). At the bottom of the wreath in block 2, to the right of

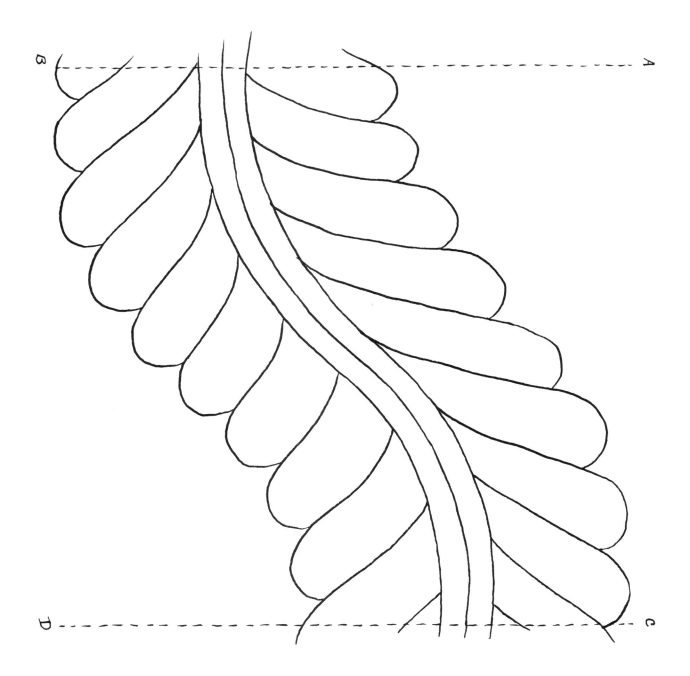

the large center rose, is a four-petaled flower which is not in the flower patterns because the quilter who appliquéd the block formed this blossom from the violet pattern G-2 by leaving off one petal. Many of the other flowers have been changed in this way, by adding or omitting shading, or perhaps by adding lines of shading in ink. When the larger elements are in place, cut out and place the simple leaf and bud shapes, the more prominent of which are labeled in the block drawings (see pages 189 and 193–94). However, each of these may be cut larger or smaller as indicated by the size of the place left for it in the design. If you are sure of your "eye for design," you might try placing the appliqué motifs within the penciled lines to please your own sense of design; this is what women did in the 1850s. The different blocks show that some needlewomen placed their elements closer together than others or used many different shapes or colors, while other women were more Spartan in their choices.

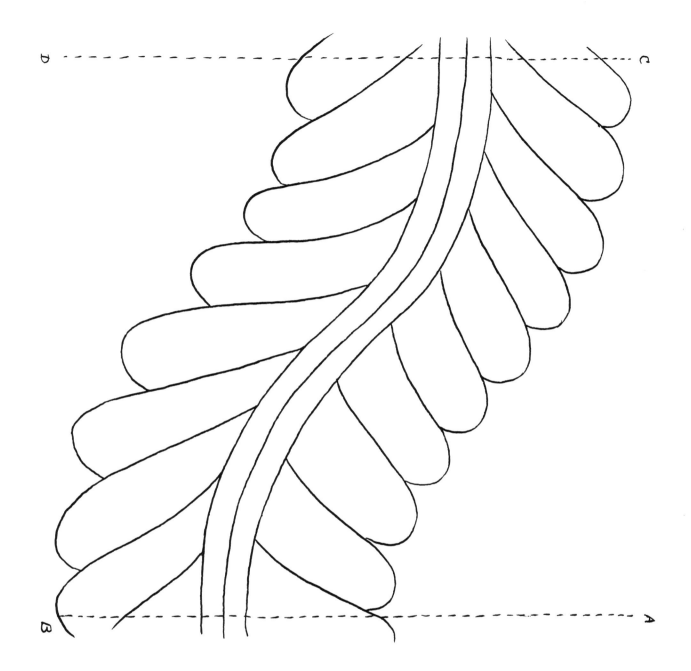

After doing one or two blocks, the differences that can be achieved by these small changes in a group of very simple patterns will begin to be apparent to you. If a true duplicate of the quilt is desired, measure the motifs and elements of the quilt-top drawing, page 159. This is a perfect scale-drawing in which one inch equals one foot.

The center designs for the wreaths were chosen by the needlewomen from illustrations in magazines, lithographs, and hand-executed drawings. They were chosen to please the person who was to receive the quilt. You may copy the exact-size patterns (pages 175–182; 196–199), or you might try appliquéing similar-sized centers in your own choice of subject to make your own one-of-a-kind American graphic quilt.

For the cornucopia blocks, use the wreath motifs numbered on the appropriate block diagrams (pages 160, 163, 166, and 169) as well as the large motifs on pages 183–185. Each ring of the cornucopia motif on page 183 is a pattern. Two blocks in this quilt use the cornucopia shape made with the solid lines. The other two blocks use the shape with the alternate pieces, indicated by the dotted lines.

To help in assembling patterns for the various blocks, the following four lists indicate the motifs used in block 1 (page 160) through block 4 (page 163):

Picture 18, Block No. 1
    Fruit...All shown on page 184.
    Cornucopia...Solid lines, page 183.
    Leaves . . . L-1, L-2-3, L-5-6, L-8-9, L-10-11, L-13-14-15, L-21, and L-23

Picture 19, Block No. 2
    Butterfly . . . 1-C
    Ship...page 175
    Flowers . . . R-2-3-4-5, G-1, G-4-5-6, G-G-15, and G-19

Buds . . . G-2-3, D-1-2-3, D-6, and D-9
Leaves . . . L-11, L-13-14-15, L-17, and L-21-22

Picture 20, Block No. 3
    Center design...page 173
    Top of wreath . . . 3-C
    Roses . . . R-1-2-3-4-5
    Flowers . . . G-1, G-10, G-19, G-2, D-4, and D-9
    Buds . . . D-1 and D-5-6

Picture 21, Block No. 4
    Cornucopia . . . solid-lined pattern for top and bottom with the dotted-lined patterns in the middle

Birds . . . B-1-2
Flowers . . . E-1, G-10, G-13-14-15, and R-1-2
Buds . . . D-7 and G-20-21
Leaves . . . L-9, L-16-17-18, and L-22-23

6

Other True Baltimore-Style Quilts

True Baltimore-style quilts were made in a narrow belt of land bordering the waterways, large and small, of the Chesapeake Bay area in Virginia, Pennsylvania, and especially in Maryland. The culture of this area was based in Baltimore. Often the people were not only friendly with others along these waterways, they were related. These were the waterfolk and tobacco farmers. Inland were the corn and wheat farmers who used horses and carts along the wagon tracks. Their quilts show that their social life and culture seldom touched that of the waterfolk. To show the substantial difference, the inland quilts were pieced in all-over patterns mostly using small triangles, while the waterfolk made quilts of appliqué, each block different. It was among these waterfolk that the Baltimore-style quilt was developed and reached the height of its beauty.

Figures 139, 140, and 141 depict some of the most characteristic motifs of the true Baltimore-style quilt designs. Shown in Figure 138 are two ribbons, the two- and three-loop bows. Also shown are a typical plum and pear in two-tone appliqué and a leaf in two-tone appliqué, although oval leaves in a single piece of material are also typical. Figure 139 shows some of the flower shapes used on these quilts. Study the two roses in a rounded arrowhead shape with centers and crescent petals. These are the two most common rose forms. The lines on the lighter rose are always drawn in ink. The three-petaled flower was used alone, but it was also often grouped in a spray of three flowers of the same size and color. This same sort of flower with four petals is also common, although it was almost always used as a single flower. The trumpet-shaped flower was used alone or in groups of two or three flowers and is almost invariably a shade of blue with a lighter blue center, although a few have yellow centers. There are

several forms of rosebuds used in these patterns but the one shown here is the most common. If the bud is outlined with short strokes of ink it is supposed to be a moss rosebud. The daisy-like flower was made with five, six, or eight petals. These flowers could be found without the darker centers appliquéd to the petals, although they were more common in the form shown. Other flowers and buds were used on these quilts, but I have shown the most common shapes that appear on almost every quilt. The rose especially is the key for identifying a true Baltimore-style quilt. If the arrowhead-shaped rose is not there, the quilt is not truly Baltimore style. Figure 140 shows the characteristic basket forms and the cornucopia. The baskets on any quilt may be a little more or quite a bit less elaborate than the two shown here. They were always done with very thin red strips. Other motifs could appear in several colors as the quilter wished, but these baskets were always red. The cornucopias could be two or three colors, there was no set color combination for them. Even the cornucopias on several blocks of the same quilt usually would not repeat the same color combinations, although, of course, they could.

The first of our Baltimore-style quilts (Picture 33) is a celebrity among Presentation quilts, for it was made for and given to a President of the United States. It was in 1849 that President Zachary Taylor made his plans to attend a fair in the city of Baltimore. In 1948, the *St. Louis Post-Dispatch* newspaper of St. Louis, Missouri, printed a picture article about the quilt. The article stated:

In 1849, President Zachary Taylor was guest of honor at a fair in Baltimore. The event caused no reverberations in history books, but it is remembered by antiquarians because of a quilt. About 25 Baltimore women had joined forces

Figure 139 Typical Baltimore-style motifs — three-looped ribbon, two-looped ribbon, two-tone fruit, and two-tone leaf.

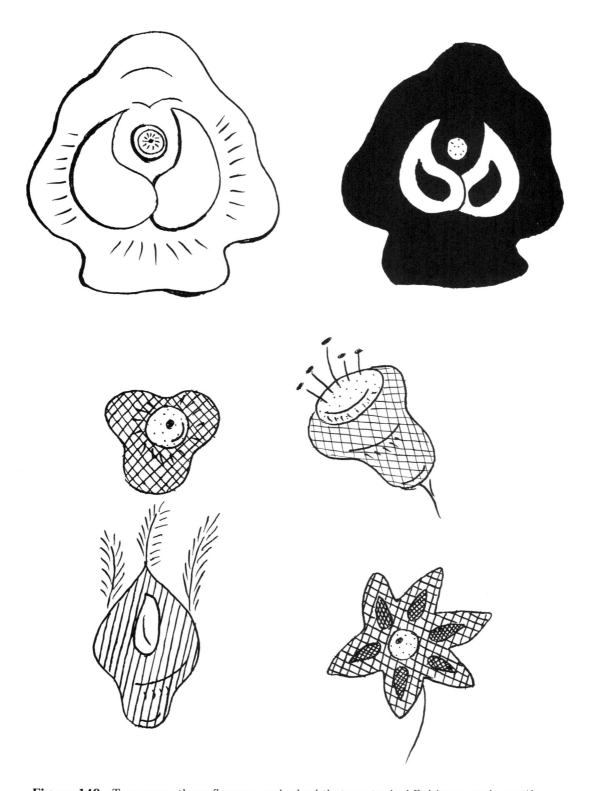

Figure 140 Two roses, three flowers, and a bud that are typical Baltimore-style motifs.

Figure 141 Two red strip-work baskets and the typical Baltimore-style cornucopia.

Picture 33   Presentation quilt made in Baltimore, Maryland, for President Zachary Taylor in 1848-1849.

the year before to create a patchwork coverlet, each contributing her most elaborate motif, as a gift for the President.

Inscribed in ink, "To Rough and Ready, Our President, 1848," it was presented at the 1849 fair and Taylor carried it back to the White House. In recent years, the quilt has been owned by a succession of antique dealers, but now is the property of Stratford Lee Morton of St. Louis, collector of Americana. It recently was the feature display of an exhibit of coverlets at City Art Museum.

I would like to know where this quilt is now. I hope it is in good hands or has been given to a museum where its beauty may be seen and appreciated.

The article states that 25 women worked on this quilt because there are 25 blocks in it. I would be very surprised if many more women had not put a few stitches in a quilt that was to be given to a popular hero and President. The center block is an eagle with flag. We have seen this eagle before. It was on the Captain Russell quilt in the last chapter, on one of the quilts in Chapter 4, and will appear on four other quilts in this chapter. If you study the blocks carefully, you will notice small differences in the designs but they are so alike that it is quite clear that they share a common origin.

The second quilt, Picture 34, is now owned by the DAR Museum in Washington, D.C. Although the DAR information states that this quilt was made in the late 19th century, I believe it is older, probably dating from the middle of the century. The names of the maker and the previous owner are unknown.

We have a different eagle in this quilt. Its head is erect, it holds a liberty cap, and the flag is at the bottom of the design. However, this eagle appears in two of the quilts in Chapter 4.

I believe the third quilt, Picture 35, is a fragment. The information given with the photo is quite scanty. It merely states that the quilt may have been started about 1840 and finished about 1865. The quilt has a large center surrounded by long narrow blocks the width of the center block. These four blocks are placed on each side of the center block. The corners between these long narrow blocks are filled with blocks half the size of the center's width. Two sides of this center and middle row are edged with more blocks of the same size as the corner blocks. The fact that only two sides have this second row persuades me that this is an unfinished top. It may have been put together and quilted by a second person when the first needlewoman was unable to finish it. The

center block is our old friend, the eagle with its head down, including the flag and shield. A wreath of roses, somewhat similar to the one around the center of the Captain Russell quilt in Chapter 5, surrounds this eagle motif. In the outer corners of this center block are small sprigs with roses and leaves. Each one of these roses seems to be a different color.

The next quilt, Picture 36, is a drawing from the Index of American Design, but I had the good fortune to locate the quilt. It was on display in the upstairs bedroom of Woodlawn Plantation, Mount Vernon, Virginia. The history says it was made in Winchester County, Maryland, even though the artist who drew the quilt labeled it Westchester County, Maryland. Neither of these names now appears in the lists of names of Maryland counties since the counties were resurveyed and renamed in the early 19th century. In the 1930s, it was owned by an antique collector in Maryland. It was found and drawn for the Index while this gentleman owned it. Later he sold it to another collector who donated it to the Woodlawn Plantation collection. This quilt consists of 25 blocks and an elaborate border.

Picture 37 shows the most interesting block in this quilt, a personalized appliqué picture. It has a house surrounded by trees and a bird flying over the roof. There is an ornamental wooden fence across the front. In front of this fence are a pair of geese, a very large brown dog, and a little girl with a basket under her arm and a bonnet on her head. She wears a modified hoopskirt and pantalettes, a costume popular for children in the years from 1840 through 1860. The third block has a full-rigged ship with all sails set and all flags flying. The most charming thing about this ship is that it sails on a spray of flowers. The border is three wide stripes of red, white, and blue material. I cannot quite make out the quilting pattern but I think it includes a simple feather, run in squares between the appliqué motifs.

The drawing from the Index of American Design shows that there were names on the quilt. When I examined it in 1970 I could not see any, thus the names must have worn off or faded in the forty years since the drawing was made for the Index. The original quilt may have been made as an Album, Medley, or Presentation quilt, but I think the hearts and doves on some of the blocks indicate that it was originally made as a Bride's quilt.

The fifth quilt in this section, Picture 38, is also a

Picture 34   Quilt top adapted from Baltimore-style quilts, late 19th century. By permission of the Museum of the Daughters of the American Revolution, Washington, D.C.

Picture 35 Baltimore-style quilt, probably a fragment, 1840-1860. Smithsonian Institution Photo No. 59334-A.

Westchester County   drawn by I. De Strange

Picture 36 Baltimore-style quilt now at Woodlawn Plantation, Mount Vernon, Virginia.
By permission of the Index of American Design, National Gallery of Art, Washington, D.C.
(Photo NYS-Te-42).

Picture 37 Block from the Woodlawn quilt showing a personal expression in the motif of a familiar scene.

drawing from the Index of American Design. It looks exactly like a photograph of a museum display of quilts. This masterful watercolor was done by Verna Tallman, a California artist of the 1930s and 1940s. It is in the De Young Museum collection in San Francisco. The information sheet says that this quilt was made by E. W. McLean of California in the late 19th century. I will not argue with this information but it is a typical Baltimore-style quilt of the early or middle 1800s. I have never heard of a quilt of this sort being made in the far West or in the last part of the 19th century. The quilt is large, eight feet by nine and one-half feet, which is between queen-size and king-size for modern beds. The white pole up the center of the drawing is a support for the display case.

The quilt in Picture 39 does not have an information sheet with it. It is a somewhat simpler version

Picture 38 Watercolor of Baltimore-style quilt in the DeYoung Museum, San Francisco. By permission of the Index of American Design, National Gallery of Art, Washington, D.C. (Photo CAL-Te-275).

Picture 39 Unfinished Baltimore-style quilt top. By permission of the Index of American Design, National Gallery of Art, Washington, D.C. (Photo VA-Te-17).

Picture 40 Unfinished drawing of a Baltimore-style quilt. By permission of the Index of American Design, National Gallery of Art, Washington, D.C. (Photo MD-Te-14).

of the typical motifs. Whether it was finished or not, it would never have been as elaborate as some of the other quilts we have studied. This is just a top that is unquilted. There are some names embroidered on each block, so it is either a Presentation or Album quilt. The designs are all balanced and the work looks as if it was well done. I wish we knew more about this quilt than we do.

The seventh and last quilt in this section, Picture 40, is again from the Index of American Design. The drawing, for some reason, was unfinished. This is a fortunate circumstance, it seems to me, because in looking at the basic parts of the design, we can pick out the important elements without distraction. As you can see, this quilt has the large center block, similar to a Medallion quilt center. This center has a wreath and basket of flowers design and a feather quilted around this. The feather wreath border in the lattice strips around the center is appliquéd and matches the feather sprays in the border. The row of individual designs in the blocks around the center are separated by feathers quilted in the lattice strips. One of these individual designs is our old friend the eagle with head down, flag and shield. The edge of the quilt is finished with an unusual appliquéd scallop border.

After looking at eight of the quilts (which I have named Baltimore-style quilts for lack of a formal name), I wonder if you agree with me that there may have been quilts made which are just as lovely, as a group, but there have never been quilts made which are lovelier.

7

Two Transition Quilts

The First Julia Thompson Quilt

One day while I was writing this, a woman with a pleasant voice called me on the telephone and asked if I were the lady interested in quilts. I said that I was and then she told me that she had a quilt that she would bring over for me to see, if I would tell her something about it. Of course, I was delighted to invite her and her quilt to my home and so, in the course of time, we spent an enjoyable afternoon together.

The quilt that Mrs. Zila Dillon Smith and her husband brought to my house that afternoon is the quilt that we will study in this section; see Picture 41. The quilt was made by Mrs. Julia Thompson, wife of Captain Thompson, a man who piloted riverboats in the middle of the last century. Mrs. Thompson traveled with her husband and lived on the riverboats, which contributed to the making of her unique quilts. This one came into the possession of the Smith family because Mrs. Thompson was born a Smith and was the paternal aunt of the present Mrs. Smith, owner of the quilt.

Miss Julia Smith was born on April 28, 1824, in Ohio. Her father, a Cincinnati fireman, was killed in the line of duty when his children were still small. The family had to be separated. When she was 15, Julia met a 40-year-old riverboat captain. They married and were said to have been very happy. They had no children, so Julia lived on the captain's boats. According to family tradition she spent her time on the boat reading medical books and papers, and fashioning quilt blocks. At least two of her quilts are still in existence. It is said that she worked on the blocks used in this first quilt over a period of 20 years, and the quilt bears this out.

After examining the quilt, I believe that some of these blocks were from the early 1840s and were of a sort usually found in New York and New Jersey. Other blocks were of the Baltimore style from the late 1840s and early 1850s. The last or newest blocks were usually found in the Midwestern quilts. Mr. Smith confirmed that Captain Thompson and his wife had sailed the rivers of the New York-New Jersey area for the first few years after their marriage, and then they moved to the waterways of the Chesapeake Bay area. Finally, they decided to return to the rivers of Ohio. Captain Thompson died there and Mrs. Thompson married a Mr. Hood. After his death she moved into the home of one of her nephews, the father of Mr. Smith. She lived there for the remainder of her long life and died at the age of 88 on May 21, 1912.

There are 13 blocks in this beautiful quilt. The NY-NJ style blocks are all red and green on white. In this quilt, there are three true Baltimore-style blocks and two more that are perhaps of this style. This leaves two that are definitely Midwestern but the two doubtful ones may also be Midwestern. I regret not being more definite on this matter but these blocks are so unusual that I cannot place them better. The two heart-shaped wreaths of green with red berries and one or three red stars are NY-NJ style blocks and are quite attractive (*See* Pictures 42 and 43). Picture 44 may be either a Baltimore-style block, an Ohio style block or perhaps Mrs. Thompson just designed it herself, which means it may be original. It has the main colors of red and green on white, but the elaborate vase motif which holds the flowers is a blue print. Picture 45 is definitely a Baltimore-style block even though it does not have the roses that are shaped like arrowheads. We may overlook this absence in the block because Mrs. Thompson was, after all, not a native of the Chesapeake Bay

Picture 41 Quilt made with blocks showing three regional variations, the first Julia Thompson quilt. By permission of Mrs. Zila Dillon Smith, owner.

area. Picture 46 will be familiar to most quilt pattern collectors. It is a red and green on white NY-NJ style pattern, although it does have a touch of yellow at the center of the quilter's roses. This is one of the forms of a familiar pattern called the President's

Wreath. It is supposed to be a pattern which was made into a quilt presented to President Lincoln.

This is the first quilt from the 19th century that I have seen with 13 blocks in it. Either Mrs. Thompson was unswayed by the usual superstitions of the

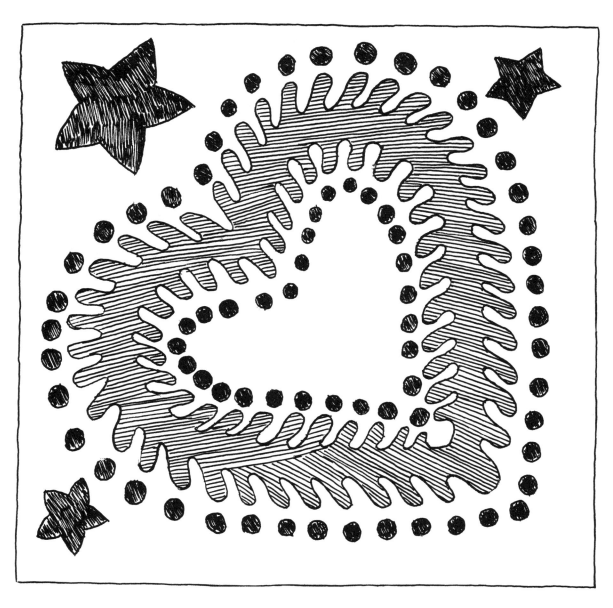

Picture 42 NY-NJ style pattern, block 1 from the first Julia Thompson quilt.

time or perhaps she worked out her own version of it.

The blocks are placed together on the bias with three-inch-wide lattice strips between them. To make this quilt a square, triangles fill in the spaces between the points of the blocks and turn the corners. The quilt does not have a border, not even a quilted one, but it is bound off in a red print bias tape strip about one inch wide. The quilting is an all-over design of rainbow-like fans; this pattern is shown in Picture 55.

The patterns for the blocks are given in full size without seam allowance. I have grouped Blocks 1 and 3 and Blocks 5 and 12 together because they have several patterns in common. To make the heart-shaped patterns in Blocks 1 and 3, draw off the two sections of pattern 1d and join them on the dotted lines C-D. When these two sections have been made into one pattern, fold the pattern in half and place the fold on the dotted lines A-B and E-F, cut the

223

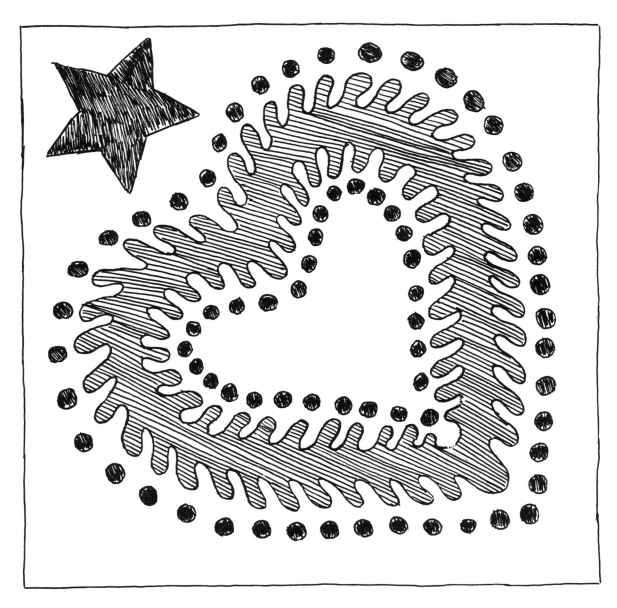

Picture 43 NY-NJ style pattern, block 3 from the first Julia Thompson quilt.

outline and you will have a complete pattern. (See Pictures 42 to 54.)

The blocks for this quilt are 17 inches square, finished size without the seam allowance. Draw and cut the triangles separately. Do not try to make them by cutting a 17-½-inch square in half because the triangles will then lack a top seam allowance. The side triangles should be 31 x 21 x 21 inches and the four corner triangles should be 17 x 11-¾ x 11-¾ inches without seam allowances.

The Second Julia Thompson Quilt

Mrs. Smith, who owned the first quilt, said that her daughter owned a second Julia Thompson quilt and she would send pictures and a description of it. This second quilt, shown in Picture 56, is now in Kansas and it is a little earlier in date than the first quilt. The blocks show the same mixture of regional styles as

Picture 44 NY-NJ style combined with a Baltimore design in the same pattern; block 2 from the first Julia Thompson quilt.

the first quilt did. This leads me to the conclusion that Mrs. Thompson made many quilt blocks and put them away. Then, when she had a home on land large enough to put up a quilt frame, she used her blocks to make quilts. She had to work this way because boat cabins, which were her first homes, are notoriously small. This quilt has only the NY-NJ and the Baltimore-style quilt blocks. The calicoes and plain colors in both of these quilts are very good

quality cloth as they show little fading or signs of wear.

There are only nine blocks in this quilt. Five are NY-NJ style blocks and two are pure Baltimore-style. The other two blocks seem to be a mixture of the two and may have been made just after Mrs. Thompson moved to Maryland. The blocks are separated by lattice strips of the white background material cut one-half as wide as the pattern blocks and set

Picture 45   Baltimore-style pattern, block 4 from the first Julia Thompson quilt.

together with white squares in the corners.

The center block is not only a Baltimore-style pattern, but also its motif is a Baltimore city landmark. The monument in this block is an almost perfect representation of the Washington Monument that stands in the heart of downtown Baltimore. It was the very first of such monuments to the "Father of our Country" built in the United States. The material used for the bird and the monument is the same brown with dark and light shading. The monument

is cut from the length of the stripes so the different elements are each a different single shade. The wreath has blue print leaves with red and pink flowerettes.

Picture 57 shows the quilting pattern. Mrs. Thompson, unlike most quilters in the 1800s, and all of the other quilters who have worked on quilts right up to the present day, did not do any outline quilting at all. Her entire quilt top has a background quilting pattern worked over it. This pattern crosses the appli-

Picture 46 NY-NJ style pattern, block 5 from the first Julia Thompson quilt.

qué without interruption on both of her quilts. On this quilt the pattern is called "Double Diamonds" because it has two lines close together rather than a single line. This pattern crosses the border strips also, ending only at the edges of the top. My guess is that this quilt was made quite early in the 1840s, although it was quilted as much as two decades later.

The patterns for this quilt follow; they are to be done on white background squares 20 inches across, finished size. The lattice strips are 10 inches by 20 inches and the corner squares are 10 inches square, without the seam allowance added. The two border strips are each five inches wide.

Picture 47 NY-NJ style pattern, block 12 from the first Julia Thompson quilt.

Picture 48 NY-NJ style pattern, block 6 from the first Julia Thompson quilt.

Picture 49 Baltimore-style pattern, block 7 from the first Julia Thompson quilt.

Picture 50 Baltimore and Midwestern style patterns combined in the same design, block 8 from the first Julia Thompson quilt.

Picture 51 NY-NJ style pattern, block 9 from the first Julia Thompson quilt.

Picture 52 Baltimore and Midwestern patterns combined in the same design, block 10 from the first Julia Thompson quilt.

Picture 53 Baltimore-style pattern, block 11 from the first Julia Thompson quilt.

Picture 54 Midwestern style pattern, block 13 from the first Julia Thompson quilt.

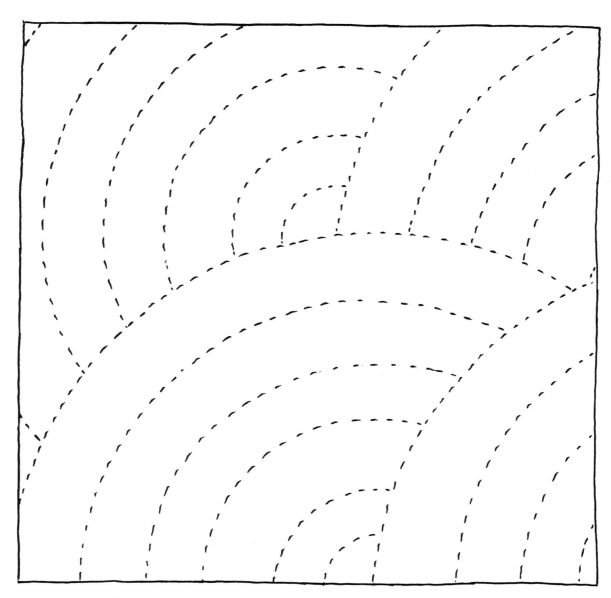

Picture 55 Quilting pattern for the first Julia Thompson quilt.

Picture 56 Second Julia Thompson quilt showing two regional styles in the blocks. By permission of Mrs. Zila Dillon Smith, owner.

238

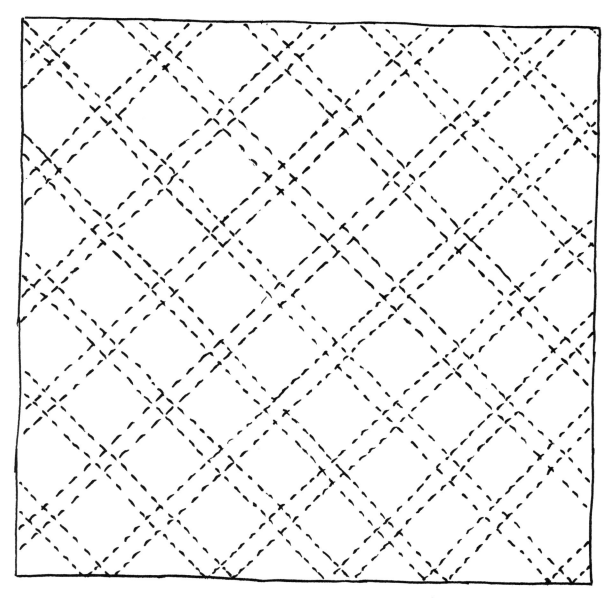

Picture 57 Quilting pattern used as an all-over design on the second Julia Thompson quilt.

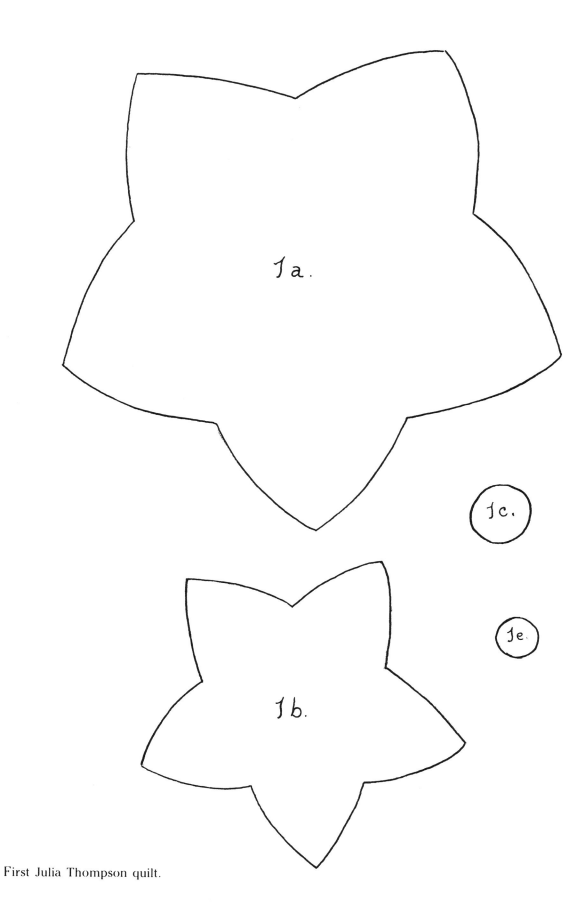

1a.

1c.

1e.

1b.

First Julia Thompson quilt.

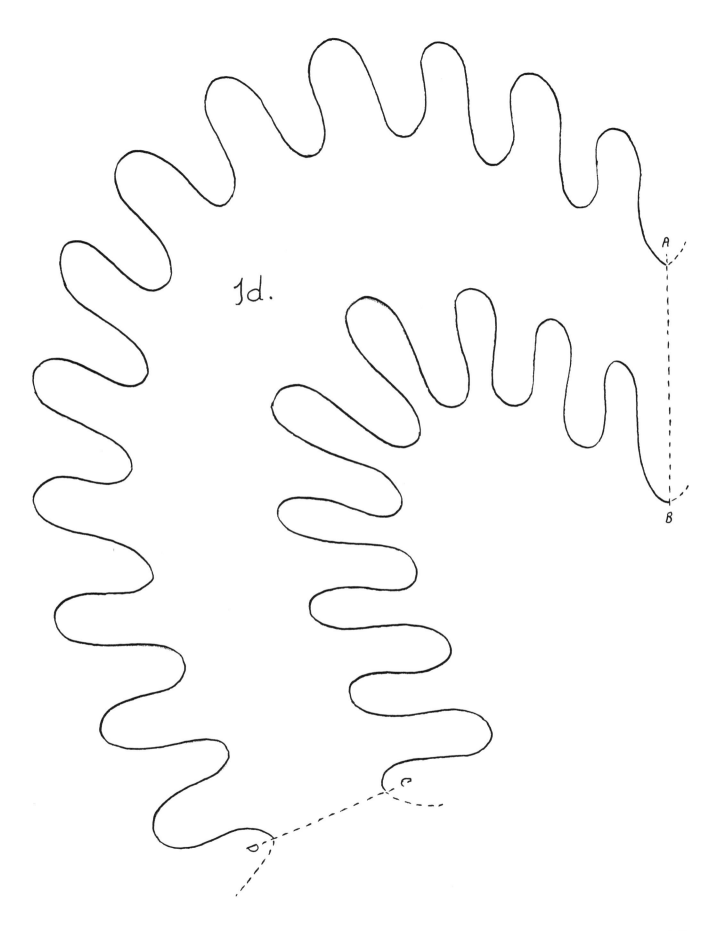

1d.

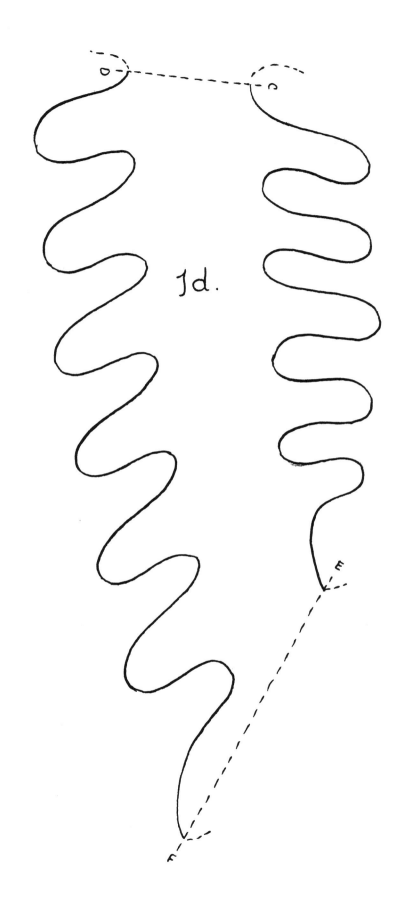

1d.

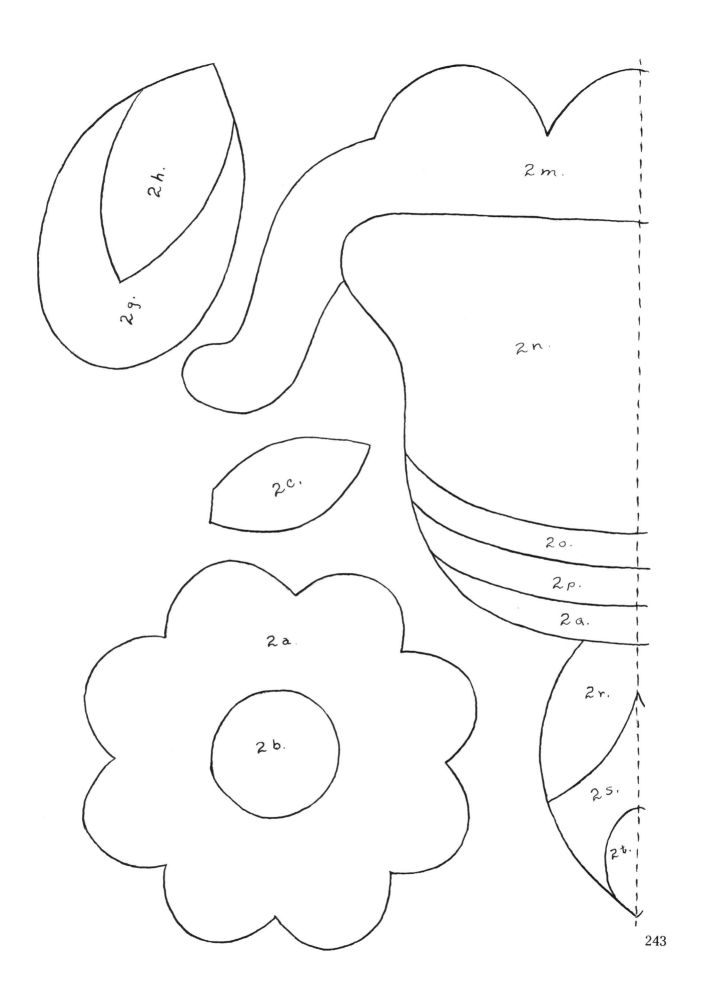

2 h.

2 g.

2 m.

2 n.

2 c.

2 o.

2 p.

2 q.

2 a.

2 b.

2 r.

2 s.

2 t.

243

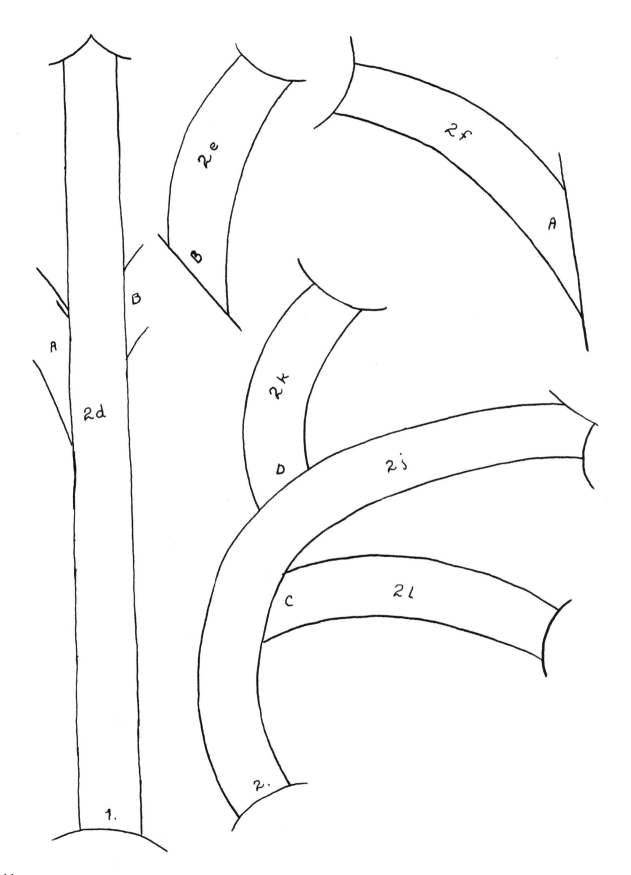

2f

A

2e

B

2k

A

B

D

2j

2d

C

2l

A

1.

2.

244

4n,

4o.

4L.

4f.

4g.

4h.

245

4 m.

12 a.

5 a.

5 b.

5 f.

5 e.

5 d.

12 b.

5 c.

6a.

6b.

6h.

6f.

6g.

6c.

A

C

D

B

6d.

6e.

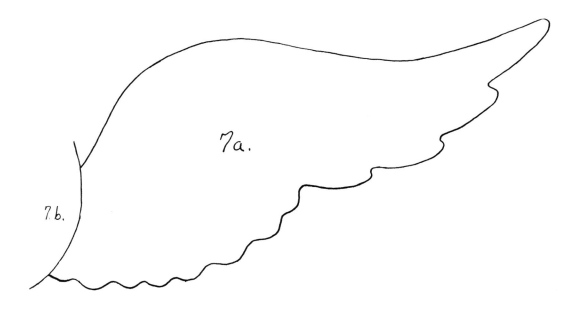

7a.

7b.

7c.

7d.

8b.

8a.

8d.

8e.

8f.

8g.

8c.

8h.

254

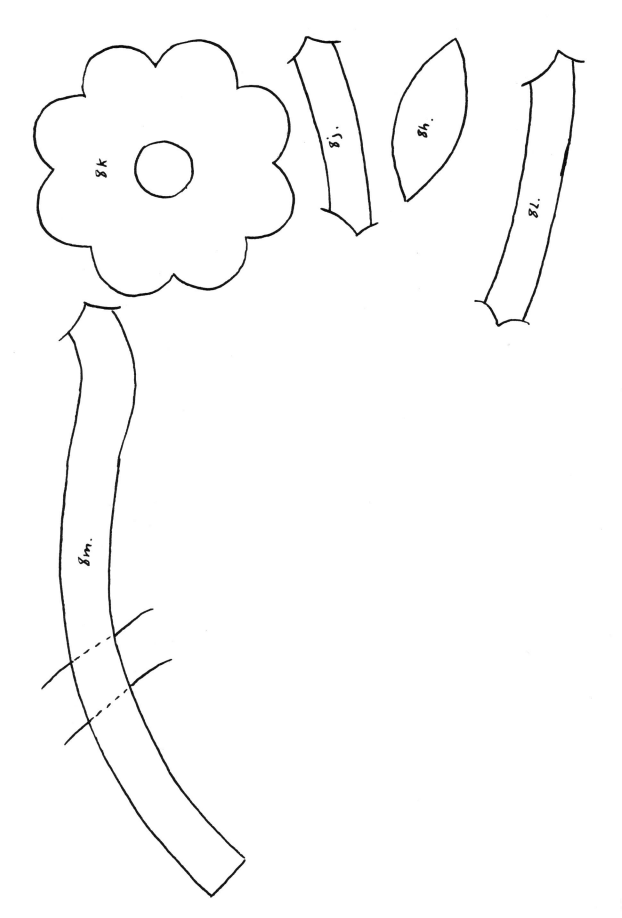

8k

8j.

8h.

8l.

8m.

255

9a.

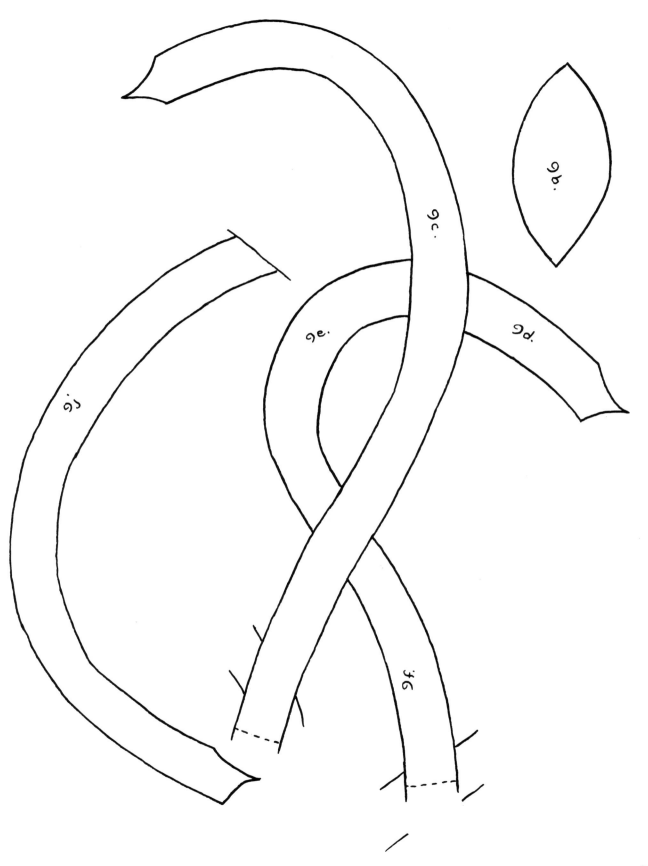

9c.

9b.

9e.

9d.

9j.

9f.

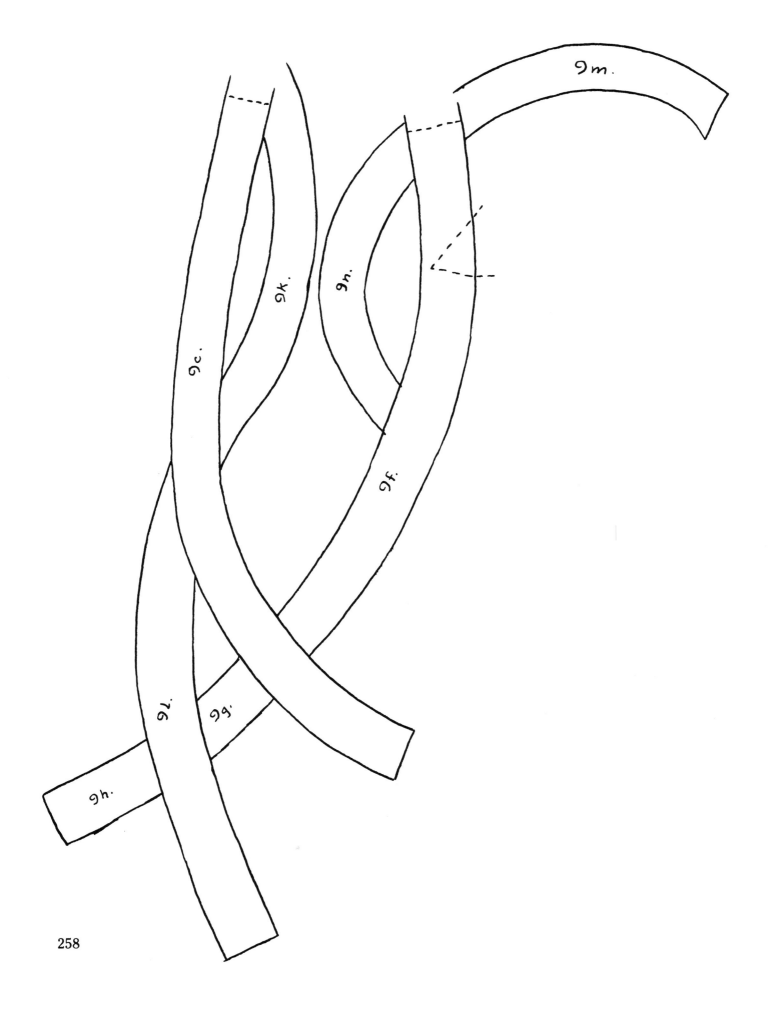

9m.

9k.

9n.

9c.

9f.

9l.

9g.

9h.

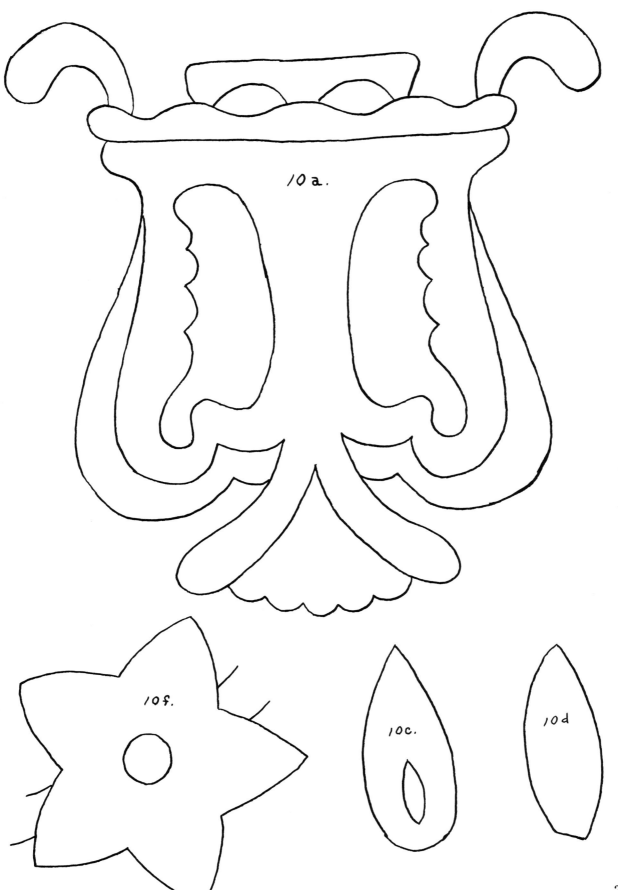

10a.

10f.

10c.

10d

259

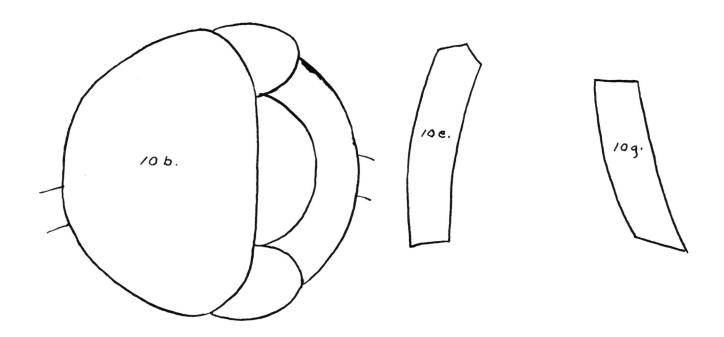

10 b.

10 e.

10 g.

260

11 m

11 s.

11 b.

11 c.

11 a.

11 f.

13c.

13a.

13e.

13d.

13j

13h.

13f.

13b.

263

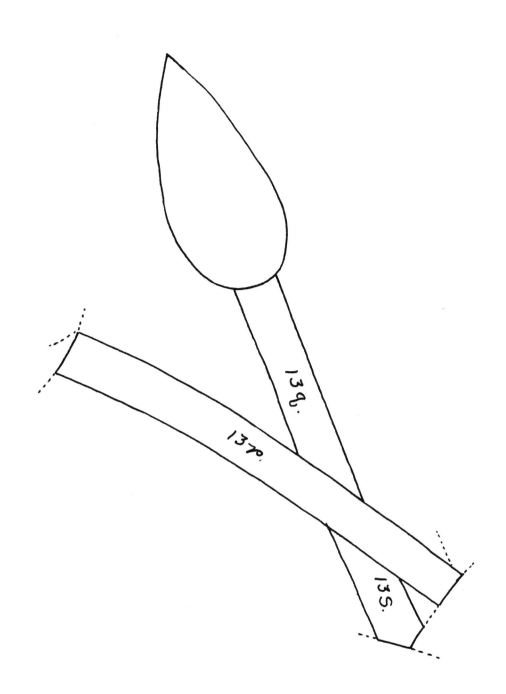

139.

137.

135.

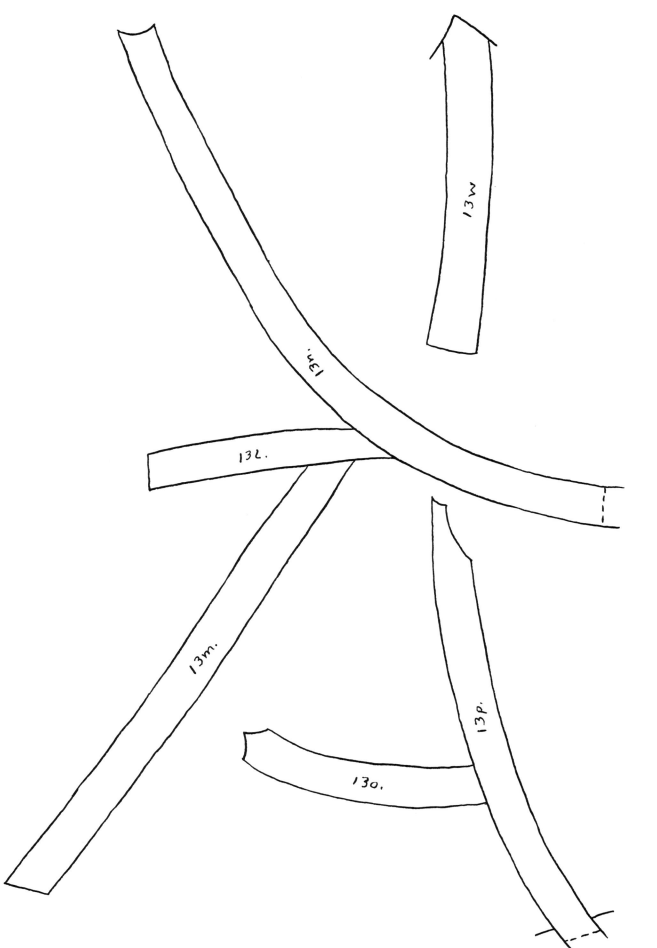

13w

13n.

13l.

13m.

13p.

13o.

265

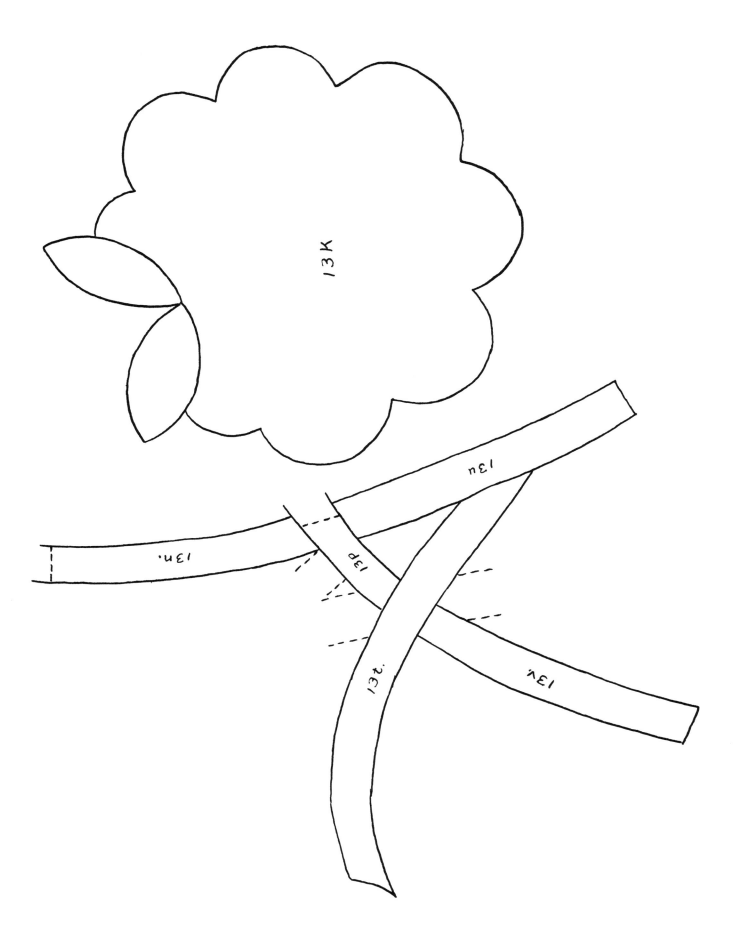

13 K

13u

13n.

13p

13t.

13v

NY-NJ style pattern, block 1 from the second Julia Thompson quilt.

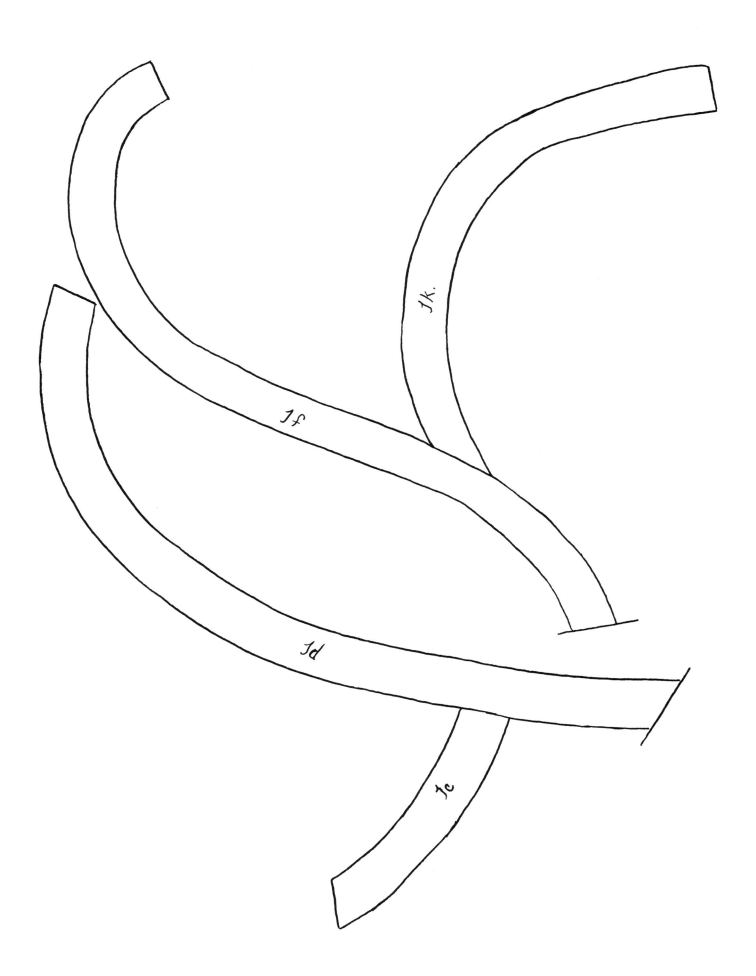

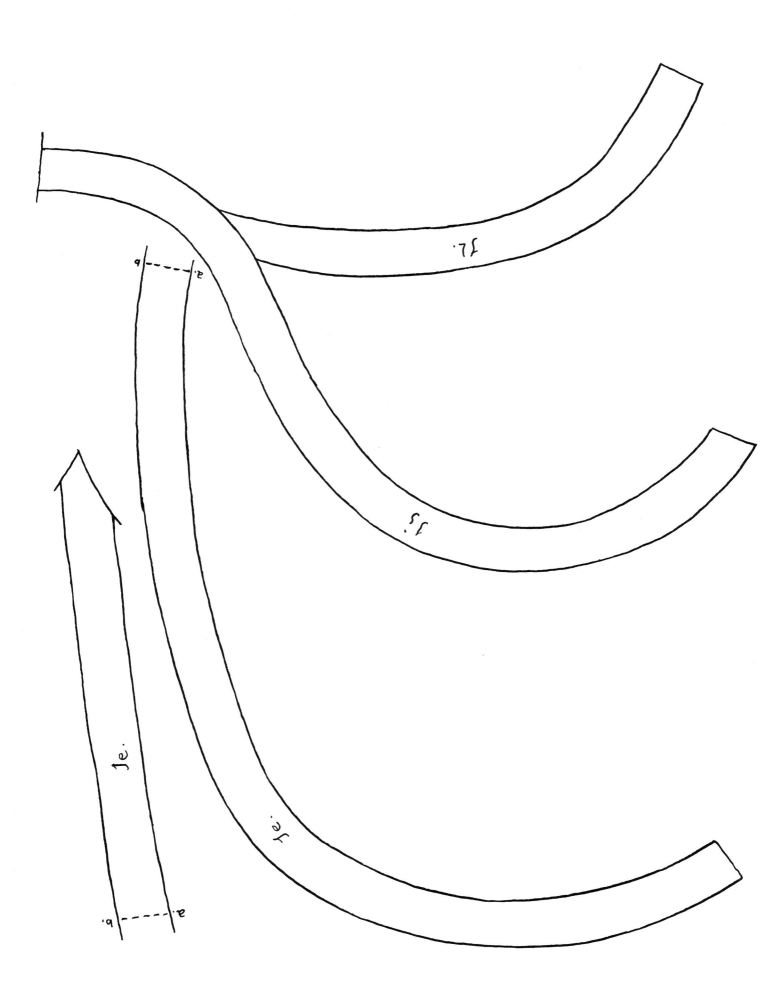

Baltimore-style pattern, block 2 from the second Julia Thompson quilt.

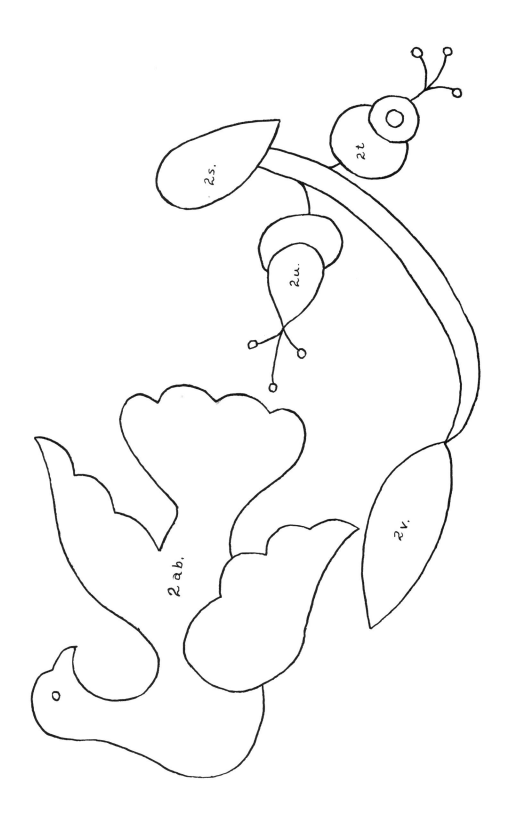

2 s.

2 t

2 u.

2 v.

2 ab.

273

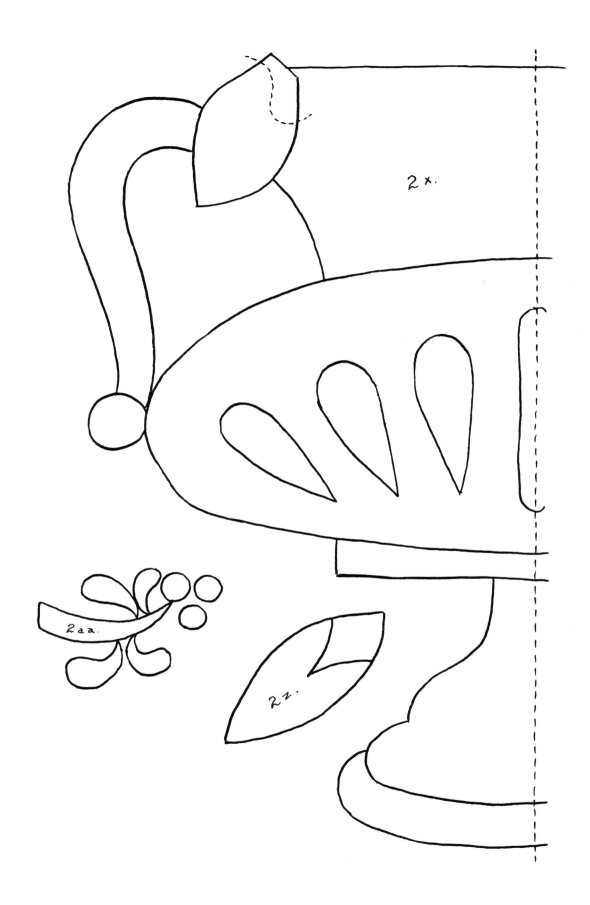

2 x.

2 a a.

2 z.

NY-NJ style pattern, block 3 from the second Julia Thompson quilt.

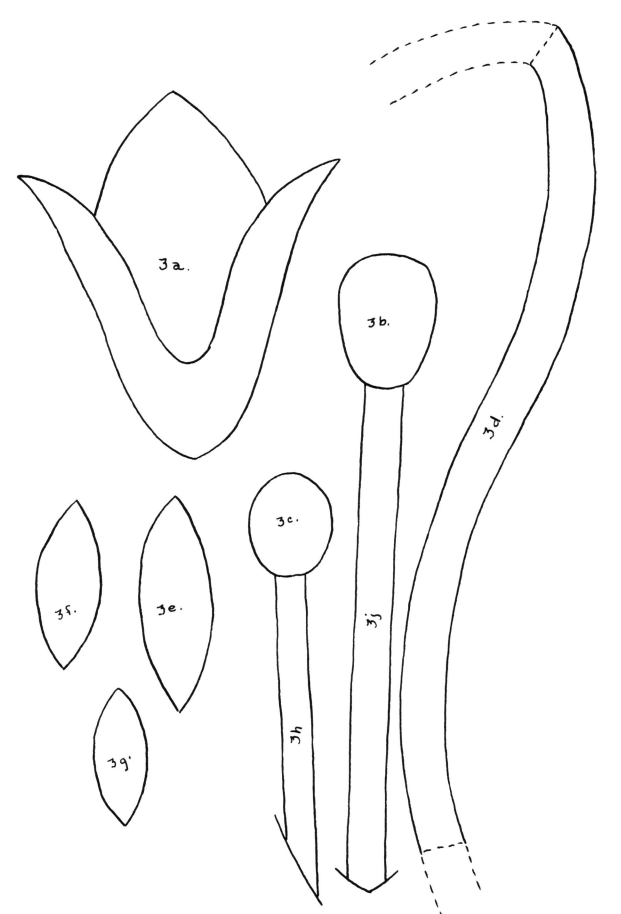

3a.

3b.

3c.

3d.

3f.

3e.

3g.

3h.

3j.

Combined NY-NJ style pattern, block 4 from the second Julia Thompson quilt.

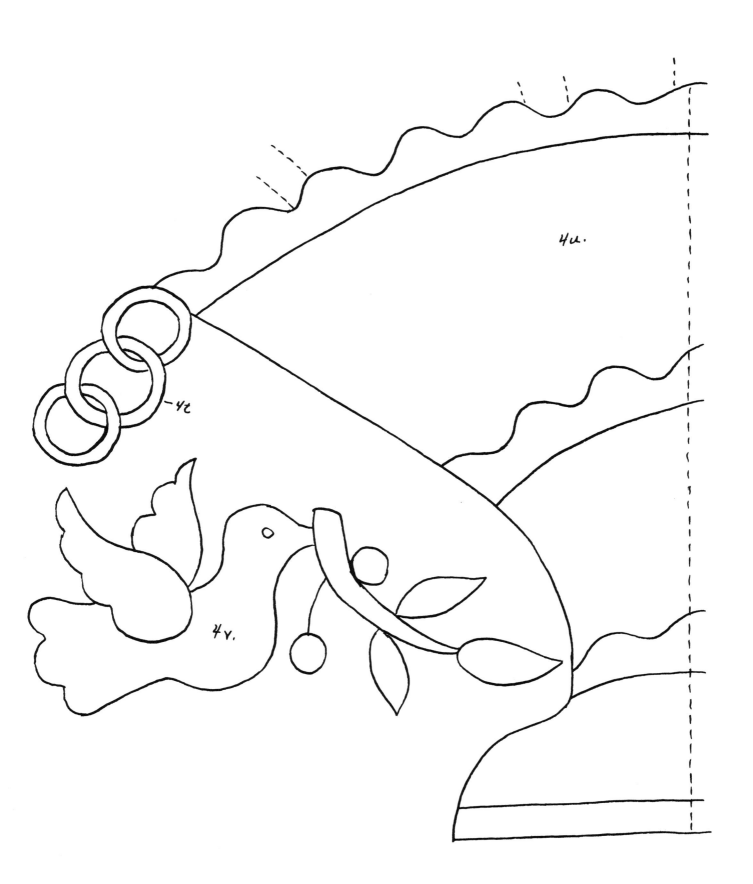

4u.

-4t

4v.

279

280

4K

4n

4g.

4m

4f.

4d.

4x

4a

281

Unusual quilt block showing the Washington Monument in downtown Baltimore in typical Baltimore-style appliqué. Block 5 from the second Julia Thompson quilt.

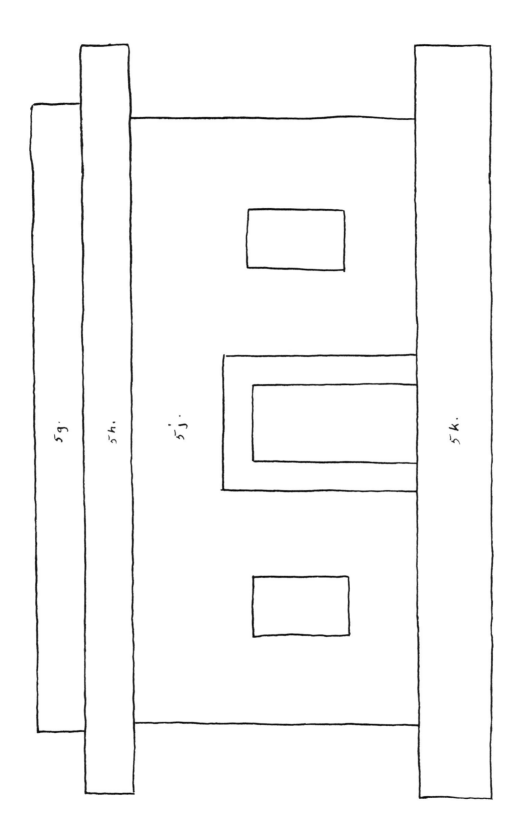

5 g.

5 h.

5 j.

5 k.

284

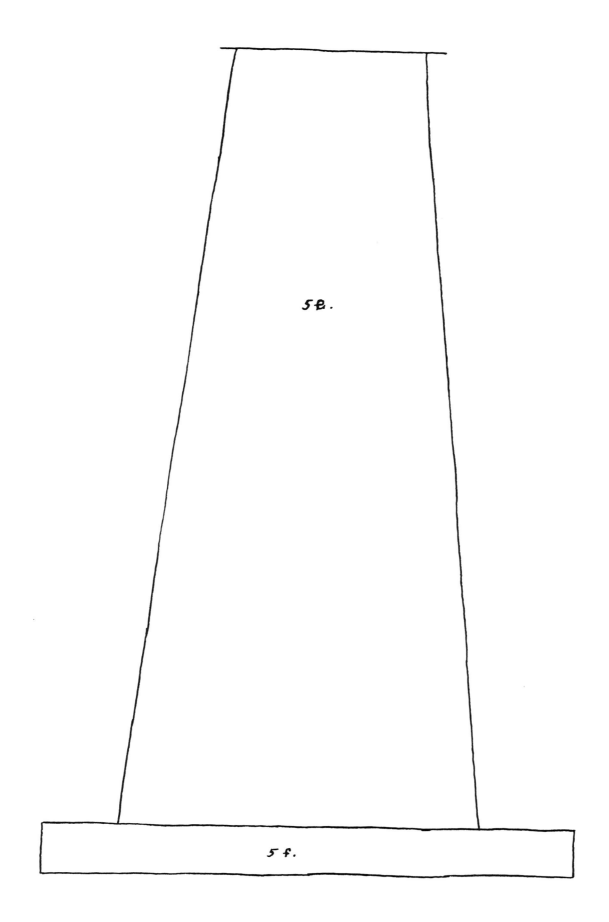

5 ₺.

5 ₣.

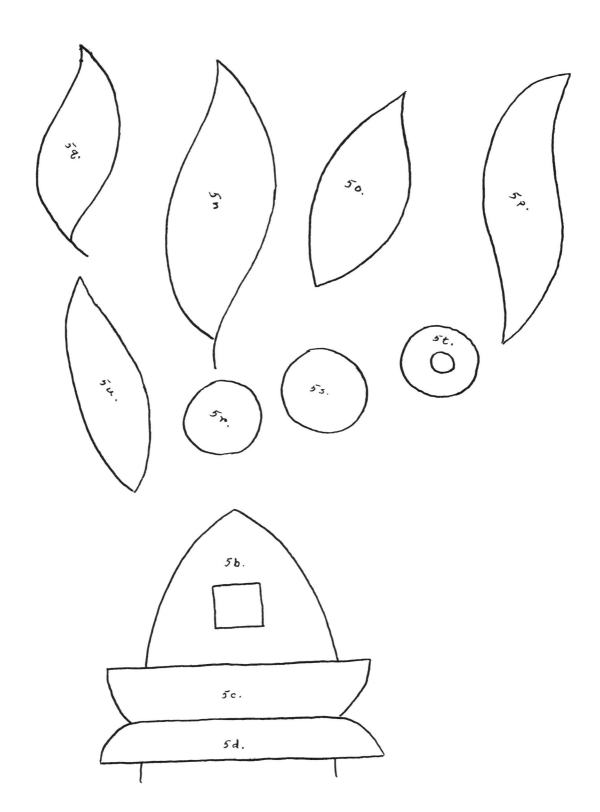

Combined NY-NJ and Baltimore-style pattern, block 6 from the Julia Thompson quilt.

6 d.

6 a.

6c.

6f

6j

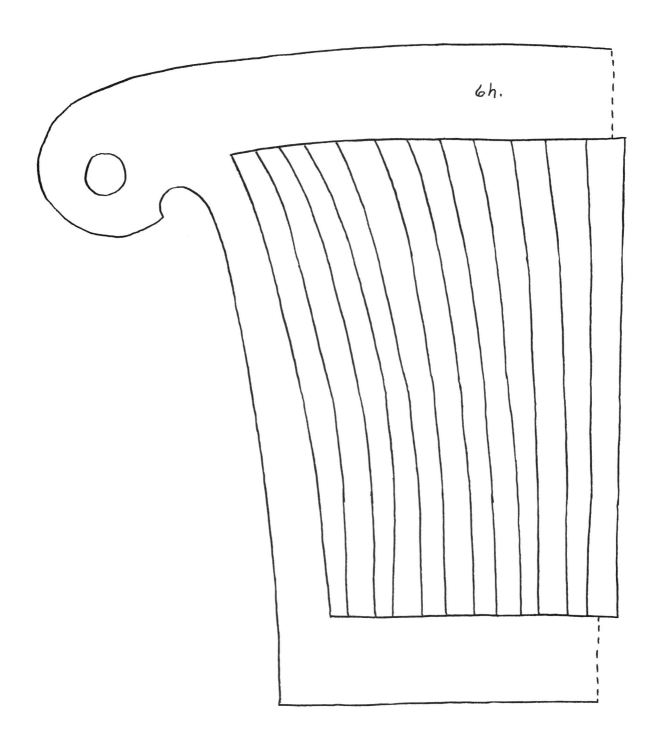

6h.

Combined NY-NJ and Baltimore-style pattern, block 7 from the second Julia Thompson quilt.

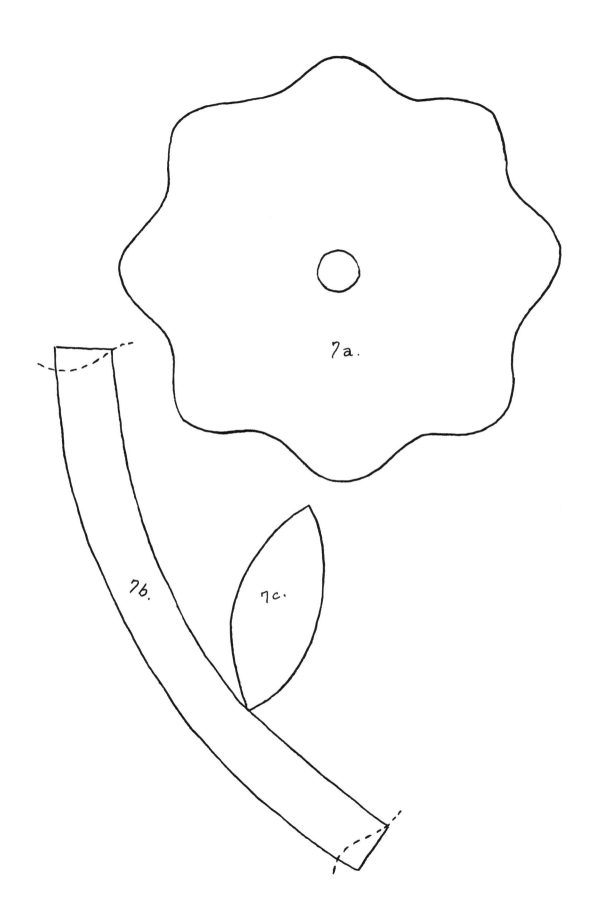

7a.

7b.

7c.

NY-NJ style pattern, block 8 from the second Julia Thompson quilt.

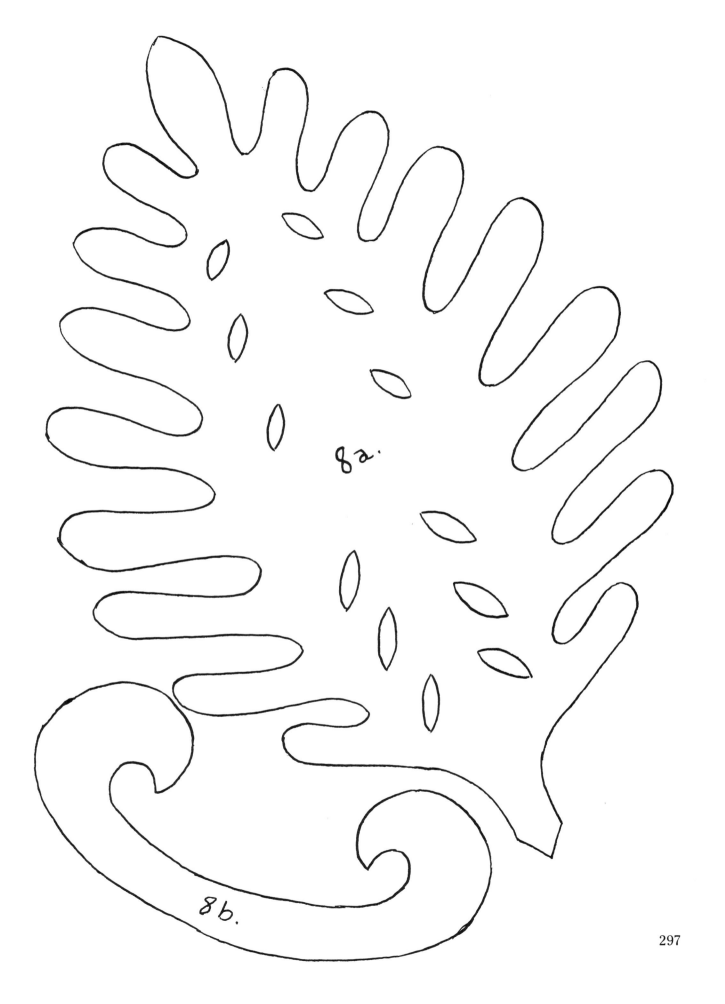

8a.

8b.

NY-NJ style pattern, block 9 from the second Julia Thompson quilt.

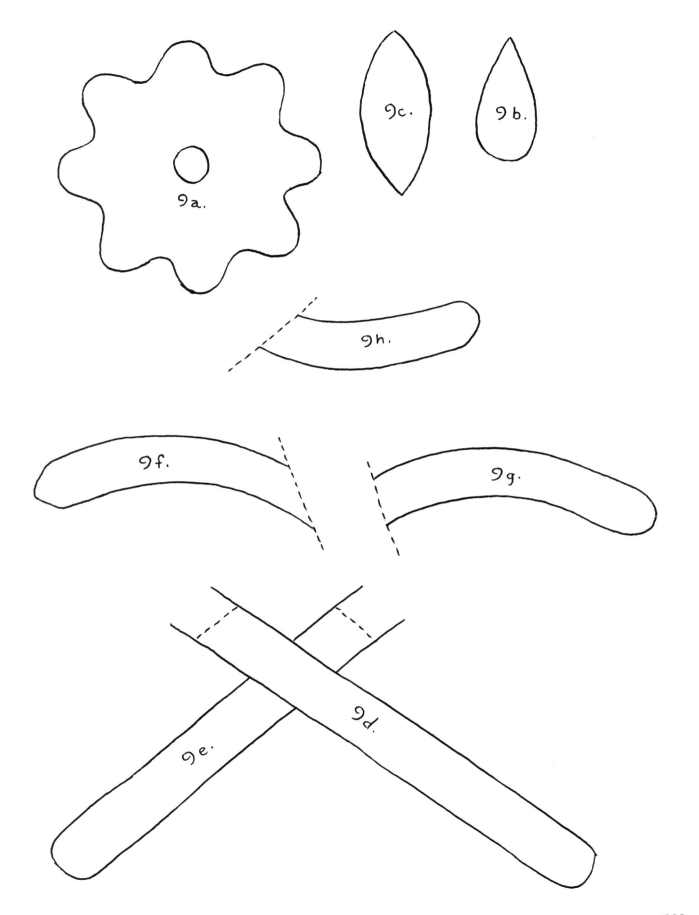

9a.

9c.

9b.

9h.

9f.

9g.

9e.

9d.

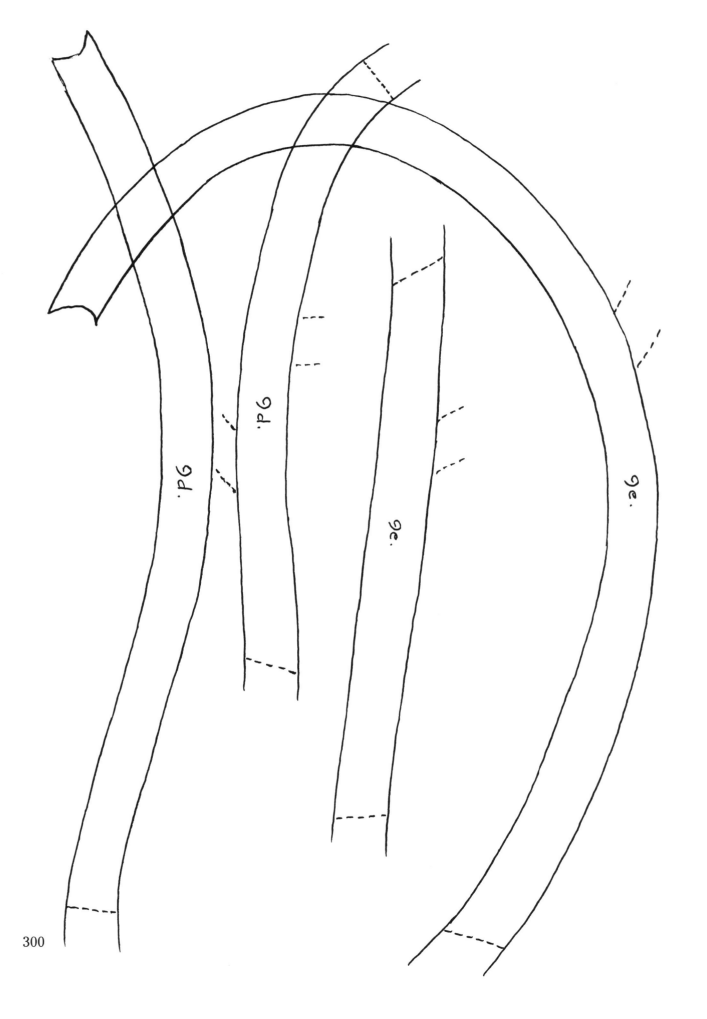

300

8

The Lincoln Quilt

On February 10, 1865, several friends and neighbors met for a party. They must have had a very good time because they left us a happy quilt. This was a working party and each person present made a block and signed it. This group was composed of real individualists, for the blocks are mostly unlike those in any other quilt I have ever examined. Seven of the blocks look like they have been copied from magazine illustrations or other pictures. Eleven blocks are common quilt patterns. Twelve blocks are of things that could be found around the house. Six are commonly thought of items, like the heart in the second block or the flag in the third block in the sixth row. The rest are mostly whimsy and must have occasioned gales of laughter. (See Picture 58.)

This quilt is now in the Shelburne Museum, in Shelburne, Vermont. When I wrote asking about the quilt the people at the museum were very gracious about answering my questions. They took much time and effort in making sure that I had all the information I needed to make this chapter an interesting one.

The quilt was found in Kingston, New York, but it is not known where the quilt was originally made. The background squares are all of homespun white cloth except for the center block, which is dark blue. The appliquéd motifs are made from wool, felt, cotton, and satin. The embroidery stitches were done in silk or wool and all the thread seems to have been black, white, brown, or tan in color while the appliqués are red, green, black, blue, and yellow. The stitches are all quite small and well done, even on the blocks signed by the men. One feels that these folks did not let having a good time interfere with good workmanship.

The present condition of the quilt is considered only fair by the museum staff, who also say that "this spread has obviously been used a great deal and was not too well cared for, in that the woolen fabrics used are quite moth-eaten. However, it still makes an interesting exhibit."

The first block is given as an "Oak Leaf Ring" by the museum, but I think it is more of a flower wreath. Block four is either a religious or an Odd Fellows symbol with the words "Faith-Hope-Charity" lettered around it. The anchor is cut out of a dark, solid-colored material, probably originally blue in color. The museum calls Block seven a "Star and Triangles" but quilters know it as the standard pieced pattern called "Feathered Star." Block nine, the Jerusalem Cherry plant, was once a very popular houseplant and is still popular in some places. Block ten is a real picture. It depicts a boy or man driving a mule. The man's face and the mule's harness are done mostly in black satin stitch embroidery, the wider places are very narrow appliqué. The mule is gray, the man's coat is green, and the remainder of the appliqué is brown.

Block eleven is by H. Pitcher. I believe this block was made by a man, and it is a framed rebus of his name. In block twelve another man, Mark Hamilton, made a lovely portrait of President Lincoln. This quilt was made just two months before President Lincoln's assassination. Another block, number twenty-two in the fourth row, is both interesting and comical. It probably represents a Republican's-eye view of the Lincoln-Douglass debates of 1858. It depicts an extremely short Stephen A. Douglass offering a very tall Abraham Lincoln a drink of water from the pitcher always available for speakers. Mr. Lincoln did not yet wear the beard which is so familiar to us. He started the beard at the end of the 1860 campaign which made him president. It is because of

Picture 58   Abraham Lincoln quilt made in New York State, 1865. From the collection of the Shelburne Museum, Shelburne, Vermont.

these two "Lincoln" blocks that this is called the Lincoln Quilt, not because it ever belonged to or was used by the president.

Block twenty-four is one of the most perfect picture blocks I have ever seen. The horse and rider are most elegant. The lady is in gray with lavender gloves and a blue feather in her black hat. She sits on a spirited black horse with white harness. In block thirty, Jennie M. Rowley appliquéd a Bible lying open to Psalms 103 and 104. Were these Jennie's favorite verses or were they meant as advice to the recipient of the quilt? Blocks thirty-three and thirty-four are closely related because they are signed in turn by "Father" and "Mother." Father signed an appliqué block featuring a bird with something in its mouth, and Mother, as mothers will, became sentimental and gave some good advice in her block. It shows a book with the words "Holy Bible" and "King James" embroidered on it and below the book the words "Holy Bible Thy Guide" and "Mother."

Block thirty-eight has an American Flag in red, white, and blue. There are 16 small stars and one large white star in the blue field of this flag. The flags of that day had 31 stars, but Jennie M. Drake could not fit so many stars into the space of the blue field without crowding. According to an article on flags owned by Mr. Boleslaw Mastai, which appeared in a 1971 *Yankee Magazine,* this flag with its large center star and thirty smaller surrounding stars was flown in the United States during the terms of Presidents Fillmore, Pierce, and Buchanan. I don't know why this earlier form was used in this block, unless Jennie M. Drake was an elderly woman who replicated the flag she was used to.

Block forty-three, the first block in the seventh row, was made by William E. Hamilton, who used a variation of the "Acorns and Oak Leaves" pattern in a red print. His acorns turned into nice, fat, red hearts though.

One of the first things I did with the information sheets from the Shelburne Museum was to sort out the last names of the signatures. They paired up as follows. Mother and father, Nellie and Larry Van, Ressa and Albert Haines, Alice E. and H. Pitcher, C. Van Hovenberg and Jenny Van H., Maria M. and Daniel G. Wyatt. These are the six married couples that seem obvious. Family groups that may include one or more married couples are the Rowley family with six members: Ely, C.H., H.C., Jennie M., Hattie

M., and Mary D. Ely Rowley Sharn should probably also be included in this group. The four members of the Drake family are William, Mrs. Sarah, Jennie M., and a lady who signed her name only as Mrs. Drake. The Hamilton family also has four members, named Mark, Mrs. J., Frank, and William E. The Allens are represented by Sarah A., M.J., and A.J. I would guess that Mrs. Van Grumbergh and Coralie A. Van Grumburg are members of the same family even though they disagree on how to spell their rather unusual name. Freddy, Coz Phebe, Mollie, Nellie, and Gurn do not clue us as much as they could have because they gave us only one name each, either their first or last. Then there are those five very unhelpful people who did not sign their names for us at all. Parish Smith, L.J. McLaughlin, M.D., and George Enderly match up nicely with Julia Risedarph, Ellen Thompson, and Laura Loucks, although we cannot match them to form the married couples they may have become. C. Mason does not help us with his sex but if he is a man, the number of men and women attending the party comes out even.

It is undeniably apparent that the above list was a close group of friends, relatives, and neighbors.

Through studying the designs used for the blocks in this quilt, I have come to the conclusion that this quilt could not have been made for a woman, thus it could not have been intended as a wedding present, as the makers would have considered the political blocks unsuitable. The only conclusion left is that this quilt was made for a man. There were three occasions when a quilt was made by 19th-century ladies for a man: at his wedding — but I have already ruled out the possibility that this quilt could have been a Bride's or thus, a Groom's quilt; as a Presentation quilt — I have ruled out this possibility also because it would have included some inscription or suitable block motif which is missing in this quilt. In the early and middle years of the 19th century, the third possibility was to give a man a Freedom quilt. This sort of quilt was made for a young man at a party which all of his friends and relatives attended on his twenty-first birthday. It symbolized that he was of age. He was now a man, ready to set out on his own, and thus needed bedcovers which belonged to him alone.

The idea that this is a young man's Freedom quilt fits everything we know about this quilt. It would explain the political and masculine motifs and the fact that some of these masculine motifs were made by the ladies as well as the men present. It explains the sentimental inscription which his mother added to her block. It would explain the clasped hands in a star which was a Civil War symbol for freedom. How I wish we knew more of the history of this quilt so we could say for sure what it was. Although there are written records about the practice of making Freedom quilts, very few samples have been definitely identified. The custom of making a young man a quilt on his twenty-first birthday died out before the 1870s ended. Thus, if this is a Freedom quilt, it is one of the last such quilts made. The lack of these quilts can be explained by the use they were given. The men took their quilts with them in covered wagons opening up the western lands. They took them to California during the Gold Rush and to the camps of the armies fighting in the Civil War. In such rough places, a quilt of mere cloth, no matter how cherished, would not have lasted long.

9

Album or Medley Quilts

In the first chapter I defined Album quilts as quilts made by a group of people. The blocks are made at home individually by single persons and then are brought to the quilting party, where they are set together into a top and quilted. A Medley quilt is one made up of the favorite patterns of one woman which she has made up into her own quilt. All the quilts in both categories are one-of-a-kind.

The first quilt, Picture 59, is a beautiful old Album quilt. I cannot tell you any more than the colors used in the quilt, which are mostly red and faded yellowish-green. The pineapple is orange, as are some of the flower centers. There are also some flowers in a pretty pink and others in a soft yellow. The background of the quilt looks like white homespun material. A very nice woman sent me the color photograph and the permission to use this quilt in the book.

I research a book for several years before I write it. Consequently, I always have several hundred photographs and information sheets on hand. Somehow, the information sheet for this quilt has become separated from its photograph; though I have looked long and hard, I cannot find it. I do not want to leave the quilt out of the book because it has several interesting features, so I am including it with apologies to the owner.

One unique feature is the border, which has a spray of dainty flowers in the corners so that the corners do not have to be turned with the swag. The patterns of the two blocks with pineapples are both a little different from the usual pineapple designs. Another unusual feature of this quilt is that unity of design is achieved by making the four corner blocks identical. This is also done in two other quilts in this chapter but it is not a design feature regularly seen in these quilts. Usually blocks in the center or around

it are made similar to balance the design of the top. The red strip-work basket in the center block, the lotus flower on the left in the same row, and the typical Baltimore-style wreath in the second block of the next row have all been seen in other quilts.

The second quilt in this chapter (Picture 60) is only a top. The picture is from the Index of American Design. There is very little information on this quilt except that the quilt was copied by Charlotte Angus in Pennsylvania. This quilt is quite different in appearance from the other quilts in this book. You must look searchingly to see that it belongs in this book because all the blocks except the four corner blocks are wreaths of very strong circular design. The tiny inset is a detail of the second wreath in the second row. The four corner blocks are eagles which are all the same. They do not unify this design because, unlike the corner motifs in the second quilt in this chapter, these corners are jarringly different in character from the designs of the remainder of the quilt.

Any one of the wreaths used in this top would make a beautiful quilt in itself and several of them look quite familiar. The pattern of the fourth wreath in the third row is called "Bud and Rose Wreath." There are a "Grape Vine" and a "Morning Glory Wreath" in the same row. This quilt does not have any names on the blocks so it must be a Medley quilt.

The quilt in Picture 61 looks like a primarily red and green on white Album quilt. It is in the collection of the Shelburne Museum and was made in 1852. The materials are not plain cloth but are prints and several different prints are used. This quilt shows a strong unity of design and I think it is quite pleasing. One odd feature of this quilt is that it seems that each woman not only made her own quilt block, but when the top was being quilted she also worked her

Picture 59 Quilt belonging to one of my readers. Quite old and unique.

own quilting pattern on her own block. Each of these blocks has its own fancy quilting pattern and its own background pattern which does not overlap onto any other block.

The most important design element in the next quilt, Picture 62, is in the quilting pattern. This picture is one of the watercolors from the Index of American Design. Irene B. Forman made her Medley Quilt in 1853 and leaves us in no doubt about it by appliquéing her name boldly in one block and the date in another. I am quite grateful to Mrs. Forman for her consideration. The appliqués in the center of each block are very small, almost too small. The large spaces in the corners of each block are filled

Picture 60 Quilt found in Pennsylvania. By permission of the Index of American Design, National Gallery of Art, Washington, D.C. (PA-Te-198).

Picture 61 Red and green Album quilt, 1852. Photo Courtesy Shelburne Museum, Shelburne, Vermont.

Picture 62 Medley quilt, 1853. By permission of the Index of American Design, National Gallery of Art, Washington, D.C. (Photo NYC-Te-246).

by over 30 small individual quilting motives which are different in each corner of a block. These designs range from a simple circle or heart to rather elaborate feather or flower designs. There are narrow lattice strips, perhaps two inches wide, between the blocks, and a four-inch-wide border around the quilt. These strips and borders are made of the white background material. A quilting border, narrow in the lattice strips and wider in the border, is worked into them. Where the lattice strips meet at the corners of the larger blocks, a small red dot about two inches across is appliquéd. Among the 54 appliqué designs in this quilt are 21 sprays of flowers, eight bouquets of flowers in vases or baskets, eight branches with fruit, four patterns with birds predominating, two trees, two men, one woman, and two buildings, one a house and the other a school or church. There are also blocks showing a flag, a horse, and two dogs. Two blocks have simple design motif. Picture 63 is a hilarious appliqué of a horse bucking its rider because of a barking dog. This block must illustrate an event that really happened. Much work and thought went into this quilt.

There are 69 blocks in the fifth quilt, Picture 64, and they were all made, it seems, by confirmed individualists. These blocks not only are of different colors, designs, and materials, but they are also made in several different sizes, so that extra strips of material had to be placed on one or two sides of some of the smaller blocks to fit them into the quilt top. This top belongs to the Smithsonian Institution and was made between 1842 and 1844. The blocks are all signed, indicating that this is an Album quilt, but I have an additional theory about it. I have seen several other sets of signed blocks made at parties in the 1840s. But these blocks were not meant to be quilts. They were "Quilter's Catalogs." In the days when cloth was far easier to obtain than paper, a quilter's catalog was the group of individual blocks that each quilter kept in her workbasket to refer to before starting a new quilt. At some of the parties given for newlyweds during the days when a bride made her own Bride's quilt, her friends made her a quilter's catalog for her new home, since her mother's catalog would no longer be available for reference. I believe someone found an old catalog composed of these blocks and did not know what it was. She then pieced the blocks together into this not very satisfactory quilt top. If you find such a set

of old blocks, all different patterns and sizes, the best way to display them is to frame each one and mount groups of them along hallways or over long pieces of furniture. They do not usually make pretty quilts when sewn together, as you can see here. These blocks were made for Mary H. Taylor of New Jersey. Many of the guests included poetry on their blocks. Notice the chintz appliqué blocks and the several near duplications. Also included are several patterns very well known to quilt pattern collectors and some never seen before or since.

The sixth quilt, Picture 65, is an Album quilt. It has 49 rather small, crowded-looking blocks which are quite spoiled by having very dark, very wide lattice strips between them. When you look at this quilt, it is hard to see past the grill made by the lattice strips, to the otherwise rather pretty designs in most of the blocks. Our old friends the lotus flower and the American flag are here. The designs are just slightly clumsier than we are used to seeing in these quilts. I believe that this quilt was made by a group of quite young quilters and this is borne out by the information sheet which says: "Appliqué Album Quilt. Made at a quilting party in Washington, D.C., for Margaret Day when she was in her teens or early twenties on her moving to Baltimore, Md. Circa 1855. 86 inches square." The quilt is so small that the blocks could only have been eight inches square with three-inch lattice strips and six-and-one-half-inch borders. The quilting is very closely done, giving a stippled look to the background.

The seventh quilt in this section, Picture 66, is neither pieced nor appliquéd. It is all embroidered in chain stitch. I included this counterpane in a book on quilts because the woman who made it used quilt-like square motifs and this only needs to be stuffed and quilted to make it a quilt. The information sheet given with the photograph from the Smithsonian Institution says: "Counterpane of chain stitch embroidery in crewel yarns or cotton. Made by Susan Adel Esputa, who copied, among other things, the flowers on her bridal parlor shades, the picture on the title page of 'Jakey's Polka,' which was her husband's first published piano piece, a lithograph, 'The Lover's Quarrel,' and other pictures. The borders are original. She made the drawings, did her own stamping, and frayed the yarns from shirt braids."

All of the pictures and fancy patterns in this quilt are exactly the kind published during the 1850s and

Picture 63 First block in Irene B. Forman's Medley quilt.

1860s in *Godey's, Petersen's,* and other ladies' magazines. The frames, lattice strips, and borders are braiding patterns used in clothing decorations. The Victorians took very narrow braid and tacked it down in these and even more elaborate patterns on all kinds of clothing, household linens, and cloth art objects. Rather than using the hard braid, Mrs. Esputa raveled it and used the softer threads. It is a lovely piece of craft work.

The eighth quilt, Picture 67, is a Bride's quilt. We can tell from the doves and the nine blocks that use hearts in their designs. The motifs in this quilt are rather loosely designed with wide areas of background showing. This is said to be a New England quilt. It is also an Album quilt because each block is marked with a name. In addition, two of the blocks have the initials of the happy couple, A.R. and G.R. The quilt is at the Shelburne Museum in

Picture 64   Odd Album quilt, from the Smithsonian Institution, Washington, D.C.

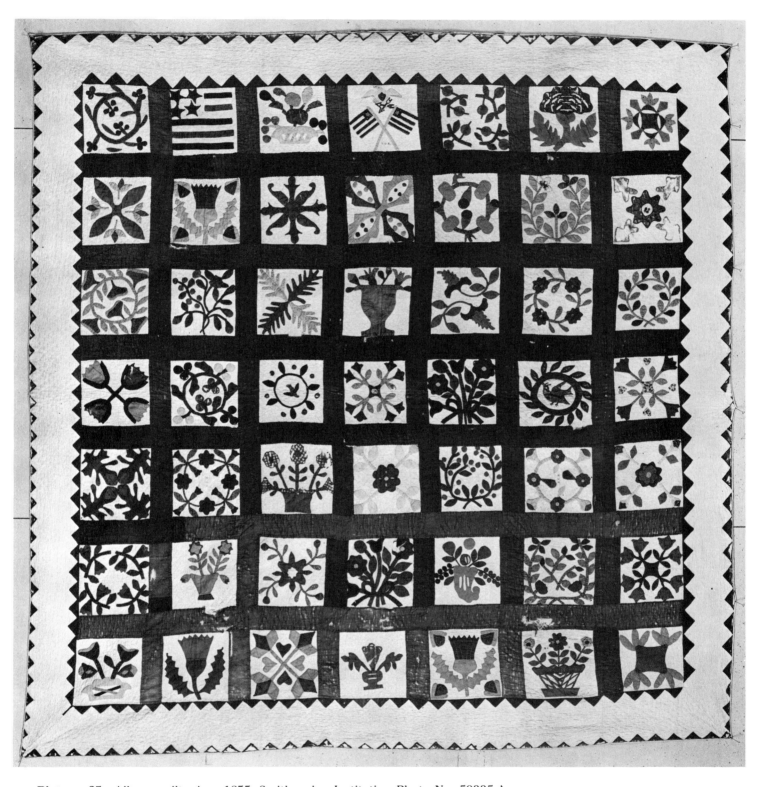

Picture 65 Album quilt, circa 1855. Smithsonian Institution Photo No. 59335-A.

Picture 66 Quilt embroidered with braiding patterns from 19th-century women's magazine patterns. Smithsonian Institution Photo No. 59335-D.

314

Picture 67 Bride's quilt. Courtesy Shelburne Museum, Shelburne, Vermont.

Vermont.

The ninth quilt, Picture 68, is also from the Shelburne Museum and has 32 fluttering birds in the blocks and appliquéd over some of the seams between blocks. Many of the patterns are symbols in this quilt. In the four corners are pineapples for hospitality. The tree-like motif in the center of the second row from the bottom is a tied shock of wheat, symbol of plenty. The bird's nest with eggs, second row from top, is a symbol of family happiness and

Picture 68 Medley quilt from the collection of the Shelburne Museum, Shelburne, Vermont.

contentment. The cornucopias with fruit are also a symbol of plenty, and the birds are, of course, an old symbol for happiness. This quilt is said to have been made in the family of Barbara Huddloser of Maryland; during the Civil War it was sold to raise money for Confederate soldiers.

The tenth quilt in this section, Picture 69, is an Odd Fellows quilt. This quilt has not one but four blocks with Odd Fellows symbols. It was not only made for an Odd Fellows member, it was made by a chapter of the ladies' organization of the order called "Rebecas." They made this quilt during the Civil War

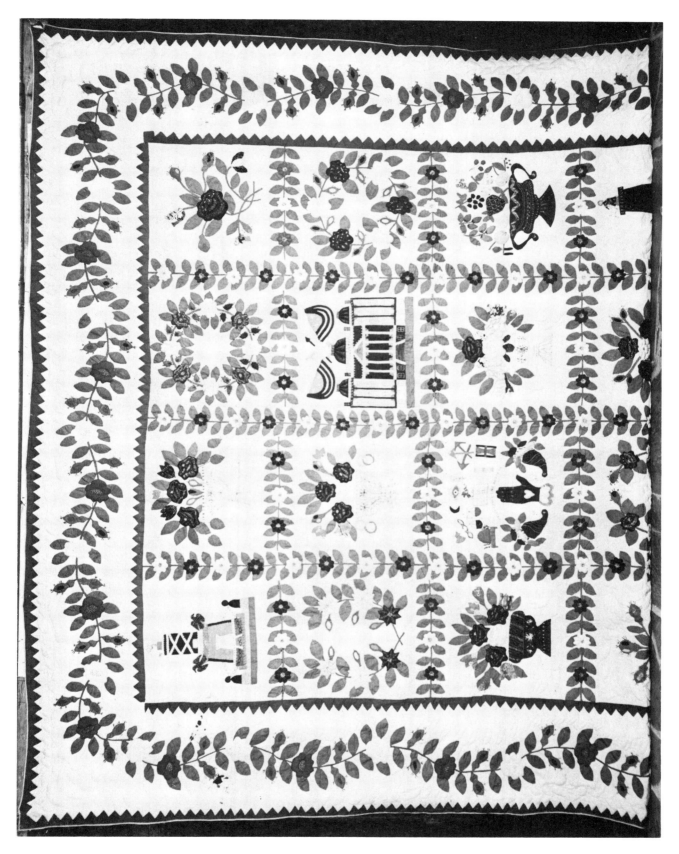

Picture 69 Odd Fellows Presentation quilt. Courtesy Shelburne Museum, Shelburne, Vermont.

for a Providence, Rhode Island, lodge, to be sold to raise money for the club's welfare work. Ballots were sold at a bazaar which gave the purchaser the right to vote for the lodge member of his choice. The winner was a Dr. M. H. Bixby. The quilt remained in his family until it was donated to the Shelburne Museum.

The first block with Odd Fellows symbols is in the first row (*See* block one in Picture 70). It has the symbols for the Rebecas and has doves of peace and other feminine symbols. The third block in the second row shows the "King's Palace," which is a symbol of "the Canton or third branch of the order" (*See* Picture 70, block three). Several of the symbols in this block have been changed over the years or are no longer used at all. The second block of the third row has a mixture of many of the well-known symbols, some of which we have seen before on some of the other quilts (*See* Picture 70, block two). Several of these are also not in use any longer in the lodges. The three-linked chain represents friendship, love, and truth. The all-seeing eye represents the omniscience of God. Also prominent on this block are an ax, Bible, hourglass, scale, three arrows, heart in hand, and hive and bees, as well as the two cornucopias. Other symbols are the motto and initials IOOF, of the organization. The last block in the fourth row represents the High Priest, "Symbol of the Encampment, or second branch of the order." This block is similar to the Rebeca block but has symbols with more masculine meanings (*See* block four of Picture 70).

The quilting is quite nice in this quilt, with the larger background spaces filled with laurel branches that have tightly stuffed leaves. The border and lattice strips have rose vines in appliqué. The popularity of the Odd Fellows organization in the 19th century may be seen when you reflect on how many of the above symbols have been used in quilts which otherwise have no connection with the Odd Fellows. This organization was one of the first secret fraternal lodges to be started in this country. Unlike the Masons and some of the other secret organizations, occupation or social status were not important for membership. So, small towns and farm areas could form lodges. Thus, the meaningful symbols became familiar in all parts of the country.

The eleventh quilt, Picture 72, is a Bible Medley quilt. It is in the style of a Picture quilt and looks rather primitive at first glance. A closer study of this quilt is very rewarding indeed, for then it reveals that there really isn't much that is primitive in this quilt. The maker was an ex-slave named Harriett (no last name known), who lived on a farm near Athens, Georgia. Harriett may have been poor, as the materials she used show, and she may have been unschooled, but she knew her Bible. She was blessed with a marvelous imagination, even if she was not trained in art. Her scenes show Adam and Eve in the Garden of Eden. If you notice, the tops of the heads in most of these figures show circular halos made of triangles. I love this first block. There is one small animal that did not reproduce well enough in any of the photographs I have of this quilt to show much more than a black eye, so I have lightly sketched in a shape for him. That urn-shaped object is a tree with two nice red apples on it. The striped animal with tiny feet is the snake before the temptation. Afterward he was deprived of his feet and condemned to crawl on his belly.

The next block shows the Angel of the Lord, pointing to tell Adam and Eve to leave the Garden; Eve throws up her hands in grief. Harriett must have decided that she had not put enough animals in this block because she later added some which overlap the lattice strips. In the next block Harriett shows God creating the sun and strewing the heavens with stars. His hair blows in the solar winds. In the fourth block comes the horror of the first murder, "Cain killing Abel." They are surrounded by Abel's sheep. Cain has the stick with blood-red appliqué on its end and Abel lies on the ground with the same blood-red appliqué streaming away to the sides of the block. The fifth block shows Mr. and Mrs. Noah and some of the animals they saved. The sixth block shows us Jacob's Ladder. Jacob lies on the ground dreaming and an angel climbs a ladder to Heaven. In the next block, Jesus is baptized by John and the Holy Spirit comes down as a very large dove. The Crucifixion is shown with the bloody red wounds of Christ, the two thieves and the three suns, which represent the three hours when the sun was dark. The two jars are probably there to hold the vinegar and water which was offered to Jesus. Harriett must not have known that the Romans mixed the two liquids together, thus she provided a jar for each. In the ninth block, Jesus ascends to Heaven; in the tenth block, the angels welcome him with rejoicing. In the

Picture 70 Four blocks from the Odd Fellows quilt showing the Odd Fellow symbols for (1) the Rebecas, (2) several symbols of the order, (3) the King's Palace, symbol of the Canton or third branch of the order, (4) the High Priest, symbol of the Encampment or second branch of the order.

319

Picture 71 Bible Picture quilt, from the Smithsonian Institution, Washington, D.C.

last block, a small Jesus the Son sits on the right hand of God the Father. The Holy Spirit stands in a skirt on the other side of Jesus. In the empty spaces, Harriett appliquéd her fancy stars and some "X" shapes which I believe she meant for flowers. The whole story of the Bible and all of its important parts are represented here in eleven economical pictures. The quilt was a recent gift to the Smithsonian Institution.

The next two quilts, Pictures 72 and 73, are both from the Index of American Design. Almost nothing is known about either of them. The twelfth quilt, Picture 72, was found in Maryland. This quilt has several

Picture 72 Maryland quilt. By permission of the Index of American Design, National Gallery of Art, Washington, D.C. (Photo MD-Te-19).

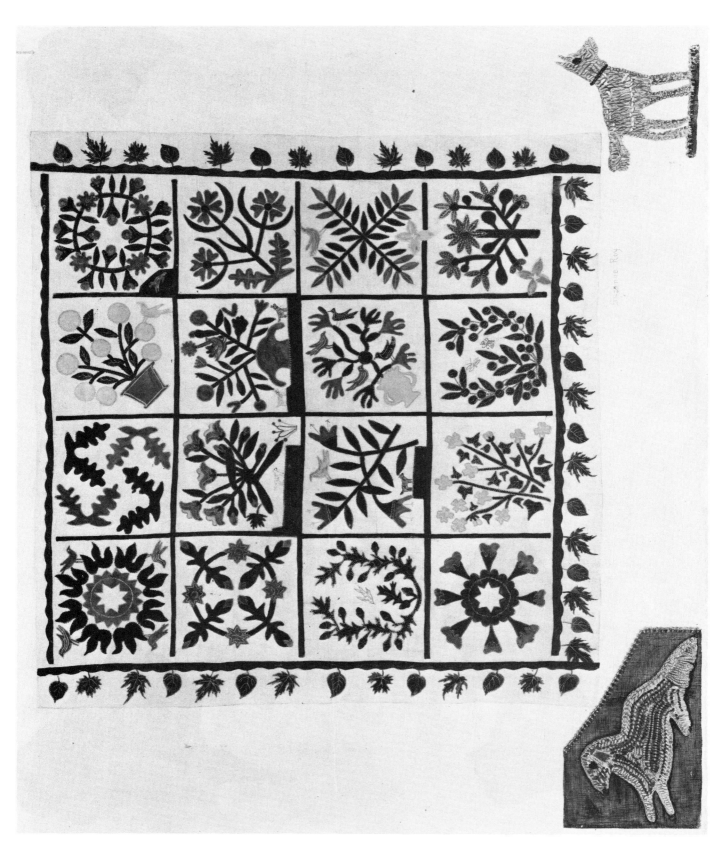

Picture 73 Quilt with small embroidered motifs. By permission of the Index of American Design, National Gallery of Art, Washington, D.C. (Photo NYC-Te-157).

Picture 74 Picture quilt from Louisville, Kentucky, 1866. By permission of the Index of American Design, National Gallery of Art, Washington, D.C. (Photo ILL-Te-49).

things in common with the design of Rachel Meyer's quilt shown in Chapter 2. The deer and butterflies are exactly like those found in Mrs. Meyer's quilt and the cat and bird are very similar. I like the border on this quilt.

The thirteenth quilt, Picture 73, has several interesting elements. The border, cut from a pattern of real leaf shapes, is one of them. Small, heavily embroidered appliqués of dogs and birds are another. These elements are so small in relationship to the other motifs on this quilt that we can be very happy that the artist who rendered this quilt made the larger drawing of two of the dogs. There are 13 birds, five dogs, and two butterflies. Both of the above quilts are Medley quilts.

I have some questions about the dating on the information sheet for the next quilt, Picture 74. The quilt is from the Index of American Design. Their information sheet states that Mrs. Benjamin Skene

of Louisville, Kentucky, made this quilt in 1866 from book illustrations copied and then appliquéd in the blocks. If you look at the motifs in this quilt, you will see the kinds of illustrations that both adult and children's books of the 1860s contained. Then if you glance at the next quilt, Picture 76, you will see a quilt from 1900. It seems to me that Mrs. Skene's quilt has far more in common with the quilts of the end of the 19th century than it does with those of the middle. The appliqués are very well done and the designs are beautiful. This is a Picture quilt and the designs do not really look like quilt block patterns. The frames give it a faintly architectural look which the next quilt also has.

The fifteenth quilt, Picture 75, is another Picture quilt. These quilts combine the much earlier Baltimore-style, Album, and Medley quilts, whose influence is evident in the block frames. The use of feather, chain, and buttonhole stitches in the em-

Picture 75   19th-century Virginia Picture quilt. Smithsonian Institution Photo No. 67629.

broidery is crazy quilt-like. This quilt shows how the two kinds of quilts combined when their original popularity had faded. These quilts were already old-fashioned when they were made. They show that the tail end of a fad usually produces artifacts which are not as pretty or as well designed as those produced in the first flowering of the fad. The picture motifs in this quilt are a little hard to make out but they may be figures cut from printed cloth. The shading on them looks a little too soft to have been

Picture 76 Modern Baltimore-style quilt made and designed by Mrs. Letha Rice in 1966.

made by embroidery. The quilt was made in Fluvanna, Virginia, in 1900 by a woman named Pocahontas Virginia Gay. True to her Virginia heritage, she placed portraits of famous Virginians such as Pocahontas, Washington, Lee, Andrew Jackson, Stonewall Jackson, and Jefferson Davis in her quilt. This is a charming quilt with its animals, flowers, and birds.

In the nearly 50 quilts shown in this book, many published for the first time, we can see the beginnings of a style, its growth and flowering, its adaptations, and finally its decline. It all happened within a 100-year time span. I think I have proved my premise that one woman could not have created the Baltimore-style quilt because, even in their purest form, quilts of this sort differ so much in style and design, one from another, that one woman could not have had all the temperaments needed to change her style so many times. Then, too, the stitches of at least one quilt prove that, although the names of a group of women appear on it, it was actually worked on by an even larger group of people.

If my purpose was simply to write down the history of a beautiful group of quilts so that I could share them with you, this book would be worth the work I have done, but I have an added purpose. It has been at least 70 years since the last of this kind of graphic quilt was made. I believe it is time for a new generation of quilters to take up the challenge of designing this sort of quilt. Quilters should combine in their own work all the beautiful quilt and quilting designs available.

I hope that every quilter who reads this book will, when finished, pick up needle, thread, and cloth to create her own American graphic quilt. You may wish to combine elements from several quilts, you may even wish to create an individual effort which owes nothing but the original inspiration to this book.

To show you a modern American graphic quilt, I have included Picture 76. There are several traditional patterns represented in this quilt and some new ones. The photograph of this quilt was sent to me by Mrs. Letha Rice of Leavenworth, Kansas. In a covering letter Mrs. Rice says:

"I made and designed this quilt in 1966. I have admired the pictures of antique quilts in books and worked out this pattern as my version of a really antique quilt. I shopped at length to find materials with the old-time look and color and then put it together. You will notice that I put the vase-basket patterns in the corners for balance and the wreaths in be-tween. The border is an old-fashioned meander with some of the flower patterns from the blocks used in it. The quilting is not elaborate, just around the pattern in the blocks and diagonals across the joining strips. I didn't want to attract attention away from the simple, old-fashioned flowers. At any rate, I showed it at the county fair where it won a second prize." This is a lovely example of an American graphic quilt and the fact that it was made in 1966 just makes it more interesting as far as I am concerned.

Another modern quilt is shown in Picture 77. It shows a new quilt top which was made in exact replica of a quilt which is quite old. The old quilt has a mysterious past. It is said to have been made by Betsy Ross, who sewed the first American flag. This is a red, white, and green quilt of a sort which should date from 1820-1850. I would assign it to the later years of that period. The information sheet says it is "Friendship Ring — 1847" but my friend Mary Schaffer says she has information that the quilt dates from the early 1830s. This quilt need not have been made by a historical personage, however; it is beautiful in its own right.

There are nine blocks in this top — three wreaths, a rose wreath, tulip wreath, two spray designs, and two identical blocks with a pot of flowers. Red lattice strips surround each block and the quilt is also bound in red. The border is a graceful vine with flowers sprouting from the center of each side and tulips sprouting from the corners. The red is a true red and the green is a soft, pale green according to the photograph I have. This replica was made by Mrs. Mary Schaffer of Flushing, Michigan. She has won many prizes for her fine quilts. This quilt was made in 1967.

Our grandmothers created beauty that we enjoy today, with just a needle and a few scraps of cloth. If future generations are to enjoy beauty from our era it is up to us to pick up our needles and cloth and begin. Making a new American graphic quilt would be a lovely way to create beauty in the present for the future.

Picture 77 Modern Baltimore-style quilt made in exact copy of a quilt said to have been made by Betsy Ross. Quilt copy made by Mrs. Mary Schaffer in 1969.